# THE
# GREEN
# GUIDE
## TO
# WALES

# THE
# GREEN
# GUIDE
## TO
# WALES

Les Lumsdon
and
Colin Speakman

First published in 1991 by
Green Print
an imprint of The Merlin Press
10 Malden Road, London NW5 3HR

ISBN 1 85425 048 5

1 2 3 4 5 6 7 8 9 10 :: 99 98 97 96 95 94 93 92 91

Phototypeset by Computerset Ltd., Harmondsworth, Middlesex

Printed in England by Biddles Ltd., Guildford, Surrey on recycled paper

# Contents

**Place names** In choosing between Welsh and 'English' place names, we have tried to follow local usage. Where Welsh names have a common English equivalent that will be found in road atlases and other literature, this is given in brackets after the Welsh name: e.g. Aberteifi (Cardigan). Where local usage favours the English names, we have retained these, as at Cardiff or St. David's.

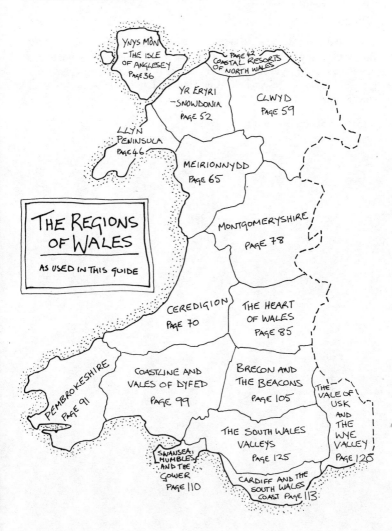

YNYS MÔN
– THE ISLE
OF ANGLESEY
Page 36

PAGE 42
COASTAL RESORTS
OF NORTH WALES

YR ERYRI
– SNOWDONIA
PAGE 52

CLWYD
PAGE 59

LLYN
PENINSULA
PAGE 46

MEIRIONNYDD
PAGE 65

THE REGIONS
OF WALES

AS USED IN THIS GUIDE

MONTGOMERYSHIRE
PAGE 78

CEREDIGION
Page 70

THE HEART
OF WALES
PAGE 85

PEMBROKESHIRE
Page 91

COASTLINE AND
VALES OF DYFED
PAGE 99

BRECON AND
THE BEACONS
PAGE 105

THE
VALE OF
USK
AND
THE
WYE
VALLEY
PAGE 120

SWANSEA,
MUMBLES,
AND THE
GOWER
PAGE 110

THE SOUTH WALES
VALLEYS
PAGE 125

CARDIFF AND THE
SOUTH WALES
COAST PAGE 113

# Acknowledgements

The authors thank Wyn Mears and his colleagues at the Wales Tourist Board, the many local tourist offices and dozens of people who responded to our letters to newspapers and local groups. In particular, we extend our grateful thanks to researchers Ann Holt and Judy Mosscrop for their contribution.

# Rhagair

Y mae creigiau Cymru ymhlith y rhai hynaf yn y byd. Fe'u ffurfiwyd, meddai'r daearegwyr, rhwng chwech a saith can miliwn o flynyddoedd yn ôl. Yn ddiweddarach, yn ystod Oes yr Iâ, fe'u herydwyd gan afonydd rhew a ysgythrodd ohonynt y cymoedd a'r dyffrynnoedd sydd mor nodweddiadol bellach o dirwedd y wlad. Yr oeddynt nid yn unig yn gadarn: yr oeddynt yn gyfoethog hefyd; a dysgodd y Cymry fanteisio ar eu cadernid a'u cyfoeth yn eu tro. Buont yn lloches i'w tywysogion; buont yn ffon bara i'w gwerin. Cloddiwyd ohonynt aur a phlwm, glo a llechi, a gadawyd arnynt yn y broses greithiau 'cynnydd'.

Yn yr un modd y mae pobl Cymru hefyd ymhlith trigolion hynaf yr ynysoedd hyn. Meddiannodd eu cyndadau Celtaidd, y Brythoniaid, Ynys Prydain oddeutu pum cant cyn Crist. Hwy oedd y bobl a wynebodd y goresgyniad Rhufeinig. Brythoneg oedd eu hiaith. Datblygodd hi yn nhreigl y canrifoedd yn Gymraeg a Chernyweg, ac wedyn – yn dilyn ymfudo mawr o dde-orllewin Prydain i Ewrop – yn Llydaweg. Yr oedd y Frythoneg yn chwaer i Oideleg, iaith Celtiaid Iwerddon, ac fe gludwyd honno yn ei thro gan oresgynnwyr o Wyddyl i Ynys Manaw a'r Alban, lle datblygodd yn Fanaweg a Gaeleg. Y mae'r Cymry hyd heddiw yn dra ymwybodol o'u treftadaeth Geltaidd. Ond gadawodd y Rhufeiniaid hefyd eu hôl arnynt. Geiriau a fenthyciwyd o Ladin i Frythoneg yw llawer o'r geiriau Cymraeg a ddefnyddir yn gyffredin heddiw, er enghraifft *pont, cadwyn* a *ffenestr*.

Y mae rhyw gymaint o ôl y Frythoneg i'w weld hyd yn oed yn Lloegr. Yr un gair, er enghraifft yw *Cymru* â *Cumbria*: daw'r ddau o'r geiriau Brythoneg *com-broges* sy'n golygu 'pobl yn byw yn yr un ardal neu'r un *fro*'. O'r gair Brythoneg *dubros* (Cymraeg *dwfr*) y daw enw'r dref Dover. A sawl enw lle yn Lloegr sy'n cynnwys yr el fennau *pen* neu *aber* neu *afon*?

Go resgyniad yr Eingliaid a'r Sacsoniaid wedi tua'r drydedd ganrif ôl Crist a erydodd yr iaith Frythoneg. Gwthiwyd yr hen Frythoniaid Rhufeinig tua'r gogledd a'r gorllewin, ac yno y bu eu cadarnleoedd. Y mae'r farddoniaeth Gymraeg gynharaf sydd gennym yn sôn am amgylchiadau yng ngogledd Lloegr a de'r Alban tua diwedd y chweched ganrif, ac yn enwi lleoedd megis Elfed a Chatraeth a Din Eidyn. Parhaodd blas Brythonaidd ar yr ardaloedd hyn am ganrifoedd. Yng Nghernyw, yn y de-orllewin, bu'r iaith Gernyweg fyw hyd y ddeunawfed ganrif. Yn raddol, fodd bynnag, fe lwyddodd y goresgynnwyr Seisnig i wahanu'r llwythau Brythonaidd. Yng Nghymru yn bennaf y cadwyd eu treftadaeth hwy.

Fe erydwyd y dreftadaeth honno'n greulon dros y canrifoedd, ac y mae rhai dyddiadau sy'n gerrig milltir pwysig: 1282, er enghraifft, pan orchfygodd Edward I, brenin Lloegr, Lywelyn II, ac y darfu am annibyniaeth wleidyddol Cymru; 1536, pan unwyd Cymru â Lloegr yn ffurfiol o dan Harri VIII; a 1847, pan gyhoeddwyd yr Adroddiad ar Addysg a argymhellai wahardd y Gymraeg o ysgolion Cymru. Un o ganlyniadau'r Adroddiad hwnnw oedd gorseddu'r Saesneg yn iaith 'cynnydd' yng Nghymru, ac fe gafodd yr un effaith ddifaol ar y Gymraeg ag a gafodd y chwyldro diwydiannol a flodeuai tua'r un adeg ar dirwedd y wlad. Ac eto, yng ngeiriau cân boblogaidd fodern, y mae'r Cymry a'u hiaith, fel y creigiau, 'yma o hyd'.

Dyna pam yr wyf mor falch o weld yn y llyfr hwn yr un pwyslais ar warchod treftadaeth ieithyddol a diwylliannol cenedl y Cymry ag ar warchod eu hamgylchfyd. Y mae gennym yng Nghymru rai o'r golygfeydd prydferth-af yn y byd; y mae gennym fywyd gwyllt sydd, nid efallai yn unigryw, ond yn amrywiol a difyr (mi wn, er enghraifft, am fwlch cul nid nepell o'm cartref y mae'n amhosibl bron teithio drwyddo heb weld barcut neu fochyn daear neu ysgyfarnog neu lwynog neu wiwer). Y mae'n bwysig gwarchod anifeiliaid ac adar, coed a blodau a phlanhigion. Ond pa synnwyr sydd yn hynny heb hefyd warchod yr iaith a roes enwau mor bersain i'r pethau hyn? Fe fu'r iaith Gymraeg fyw'n naturiol yn ei hamgylchfyd am bedair canrif ar ddeg, ac ni ellir gwahanu'r naill oddi wrth y llall.

Harddu yn araf y mae Cymru'r dyddiau hyn, gyda diflaniad llawer o'i hen weithfeydd myglyd a thirlunio o'r newydd ei hen dipiau glo a'i thomenni llechi. Does dim dwywaith nad yw ei hamgylchfyd mewn llawer lle yn lanach a mwy dymunol nag y bu. Ochr arall y geiniog, wrth gwrs, yw'r effaith a gaiff hyn ar y cymunedau a ddibynnai ar yr hen ddiwydiannau. Wedi'r cyfan, y mae dadfeiliad diwydiant yn arwain yn aml i ddiweithdra a diboblogi. Sonia un o hen chwedlau'r Mabinogi, a ysgrifennwyd tua'r ddeuddegfed ganrif, am niwl hud yn disgyn ar y wlad, a phan gododd yr oedd ei phobl oll wedi diflannu. Ymddengys mai'r her i ni yn yr unfed ganrif ar hugain fydd gwarchod ein hamgylchedd a darparu ar yr un pryd ddulliau i gynnal ein cymunedau ac i warchod eu ffordd o fyw.

Yng ngwaelod yr ardd yng nghefn fy nhŷ y mae afon fechan – afon Crewi. Dywedir wrthyf na fu pysgod yn yr afon honno am flynyddoedd lawer. Yr oedd gwaith mwyn Dylife yn y bryniau uwchben wedi llygru'r dŵr a'i gwneud hi'n amhosibl i ddim fyw ynddo. Ond droeon yn ystod y blynyddoedd diwethaf hyn fe welais grëyr glas yn hedfan i fyny'r afon (i 'agor y fflodiat', meddai'r hen bobl – 'arwydd glaw'), ac y mae hynny i mi yn awgrymu bod y pysgod yn dechrau dod yn eu hôl. Fel yna, yn raddol, yr adferir yr amgylchfyd, a'r iaith, yng Nghymru. Rhaid inni ddysgu o'r newydd sut i barchu creadigaeth Duw yn ei hamrywiaeth gyfoethog.

Un cam tuag at hynny yw cyhoeddi'r llyfr hwn. Fy mraint i yw cael ei gymeradwyo.

Gwynn ap Gwilym
Penegoes
Medi 1990

# Foreword

The rocks of Wales are amongst the most ancient in the world. Geologists maintain that they were formed some six or seven hundred million years ago. Later, during the Ice Age, they were eroded by glaciers which carved out of them the cwms and valleys which are now so typical of the country's landscape. They were not only firm: they were also rich; and the Welsh people learnt how to take advantage of both their might and their wealth. They provided shelter for the princes; they provided a living for the people. Gold and lead, coal and slate were mined out of them, and left them bearing the scars of 'progress'.

The Welsh people too are among the most ancient inhabitants of these islands. Their Celtic forefathers, the Britons, took possession of the Isle of Britain some five centuries before Christ. They were the people who faced the Roman invasion. Their language was Brythonic, which in time developed into Welsh and Cornish, and then – following a large migration from south-west Britain to Europe – into Breton. Brythonic had a sister language, Goidelic, the language of the Irish Celts, which in turn was taken by Irish settlers to the Isle of Man and Scotland where it developed into Manx and Scots Gaelic. The Welsh are still very conscious of their Celtic heritage. They were influenced also, however, by the Romans. Many Welsh words in common usage today are Latin loan words, for example *pont* (bridge), *cadwyn* (chain), *ffenestr* (window).

Brythonic has left its mark even on England. *Cumbria*, for instance, is the same word as *Cymru* (Wales): both are derived from the Brythonic words *com-broges*, which means 'people living in the same district' (*bro*). The place-name *Dover* is derived from Brythonic *dubros* (Welsh *dwfr* = water). And how many place-names in England contain the elements *pen* (head), *aber* (estuary) or *afon* (river)?

It was the invasion of the Angles and Saxons after the third century AD that eroded the Brythonic language. The ancient Roman Britons were pushed to the north and to the west, and established there their strongholds. The oldest Welsh poetry extant speaks of conditions in the north of England and the south of Scotland towards the end of the sixth century, and mentions places such as Elfed (Elmet), Catraeth (Catterick) and Din Eidyn (Edinburgh). These areas preserved their Brythonic character for centuries. In Cornwall, in the south-west, the Cornish language lived until the eighteenth century. Gradually, however, the English invaders succeeded in destroying the unity of the Brythonic tribes. It was in Wales, more than any other region, that the Brythonic heritage was preserved.

Over the centuries that heritage was cruelly eroded, and there are some dates which are important milestones: 1282, for instance, when Edward I, king of England, conquered Llywelyn II, thereby quashing the political independence of Wales; 1536, when Wales was formally annexed to England under Henry VIII; and 1847, when a Report on Education recommended that the Welsh language be banished from the schools of Wales. One of the results of that report was to establish English as the language of 'progress' in Wales, and it had the same destructive effect on Welsh as did the industrial revolution, which flourished around the same time, on the country's landscape. And yet, in the words of a modern pop song, the Welsh people and their language, like the rocks, are 'still here'.

That is why I was so glad to see in this book the same emphasis laid on the preservation of the linguistic and cultural heritage of the Welsh nation as on the preservation of its environment. In Wales we have some of the best scenery in the world; we have a wildlife which, although not unique, is varied and interesting (I know, for instance, of a narrow pass not far away from my home through which it is virtually impossible to travel without seeing a kite, a badger, a hare, a fox or a squirrel). It is important to preserve animals and birds, trees, flowers and plants. But what sense is there in that without also preserving the language that has given to these things such sweet-sounding names? The Welsh language has lived naturally in its environment for fourteen centuries, and is inseparable from it.

Wales nowadays, with the demise of many of its smoky industries and the new landscaping of its old coal and slate tips, is gradually becoming more beautiful. Its environment is without doubt cleaner and more pleasant than it used to be. The other side of the coin, of course, is the effect that all this has on the communities that were dependent on these old industries. After all, the loss of industry often leads to unemployment and depopulation. One of the tales of the Mabinogi, written around the twelfth century, speaks of a magic mist descending on the countryside, and, when the mist lifted, all the people had vanished. It would seem that the challenge facing us in the twenty-first century is to preserve our environment whilst at the same time providing the means to sustain our communities and their way of life.

At the bottom of the garden behind my house there is a small river – the River Crewi. I am told that for a great many years there were no fish in that river. The lead mines of Dylife in the hills above had polluted the water, making it impossible for anything to live in it. Yet, several times in these few years past I have seen a heron flying up the river (to 'open the flood-gates', say the old people – 'a sign of rain'), and this to me suggests that the fish are gradually returning. It is in this manner – gradually – that the environment, and the language, will be restored in Wales. We must learn anew how to respect the rich variety of God's creation.

One step towards that goal is the publication of this book. It is my privilege to recommend it.

Gwynn ap Gwilym<br>Penegoes, September 1990

# PART 1:
# A GREEN INTRODUCTION TO WALES

# How to use this book

The Green Guide to Wales, like the earlier Green Guide to England and Green Guide to Scotland, offers an alternative way of getting to know Britain. It suggests what we hope will prove a wide choice of experiences of this most beautiful and distinctive land. However, it is not just another guide; it questions many of the traditionally held views about tourism and it searches out a Green approach to travel.

For tourism should be a two-way process. Passive absorption of a landscape and a culture in which scenery flits past the windscreen of a car is not the experience envisaged in this book. There is a different approach, which encourages a dialogue between visitor and host, where speed is not the essence and which above all is less exacting on our environment.

Of course you can 'do' Wales in a day if you want to, driving at fairly high speeds from Cardiff to Holyhead and off again to Chester, collecting 'sights' en route and just pausing long enough at a service station to buy a tacky windscreen sticker of that Welsh dragon. Surely this is not what being a visitor in a lovely country should be like and this book explains how to avoid the trap.

So who is this guide for?

Below we try to define the Green traveller as someone who not only takes pleasures, experiences and memories from the place he or she visits, but tries to give something back in return, and in so doing has a deeper, richer and rather more fulfilling experience of Wales than the passive visitor can even begin to comprehend.

This book is for such people.

Having defined, as it were, the ground rules and the perspectives, we look at Wales in terms of its unique and special sense of place. This begins with an overview of Wales from these perspectives and some practical advice – because this has to be a practical book – on where to start.

We then look in more detail at the landscape and some of the forces, natural and human, that have shaped that landscape. Welsh people dominate the next chapter, and we look at Welshness in a Welsh, British and European context, and at the history of the Welsh nation and its long and continuing struggle to retain its unique identity.

Then follow two practical sections which first of all illustrate how you can enjoy even remote rural Wales without having to pollute the planet excessively, and secondly, having got you around, offer some advice on where to stay and the enjoyment of Welsh cuisine, with an emphasis on wholefood and organically-farmed food.

Part Two looks at the regions of Wales in greater detail, and highlights some of the very many opportunities available for what in the Alpine countries is becoming known as the 'new tourism'.

Wherever possible we support each of our regional sections by suggestions for further reading and research. One problem is that for small businesses and enterprises, Green ones included, survival is sometimes hazardous, and changes are inevitable. Where places are off the beaten track we have listed the telephone numbers in the text. A phone call before a planned visit might be wise, to ensure facilities or opening times have not changed. Tourist Information Offices and voluntary groups can be marvellous providers of up-to-date information and once you are plugged into a network you will soon find more information.

Appreciate too that a book of this nature can be no more than an introduction to a land as complex, rich and varied as Wales. We took the decision not to attempt to include everything, nor to knock examples of the unsympathetic or 'hard' tourism, including the large ugly seaside caravan sites, the glitzy theme parks and timeshare developments. Wales, like everywhere else, has its share of these. In fact there is an argument that cheeky and cheerful honeypot places do a great job in absorbing lots of people in fairly small areas, rather than spreading them out into more vulnerable areas of countryside. But because this book is a 'Green Guide' it is not about those places.

Inevitably there will be inaccuracies; things can and do change so quickly. If you come across new information or new projects that you feel merit inclusion in a future edition of this guide, please use the form at the end of this book or write to us.

# The regional sections

In Part Two of this book you will find Wales broken down into geographical sections, in a similar format to Wales Tourist Board official brochures and accommodation guides. This should make cross-reference with other brochures and booklets easier.

Information regarding attractions and groups includes telephone numbers wherever known and also relevant access information where feasible.

Attractions expressing an interest in interpreting the countryside or aspects of the countryside are included; there is a wide range of facilities, from a true working farm or mill to something far more geared to the visitor. We have not, however, listed the dozens of pony-trekking centres throughout Wales – see the Wales Tourist Board booklets for details.

In terms of crafts we have endeavoured to feature those places where visitors are welcome on a regular basis and where craft skills are demonstrated and the products of these skills sold.

The inclusion of wholefood shops and eating places is by no means comprehensive, but we have highlighted at least those places known to us or to colleagues which offer good food, sometimes meat as well as vegetarian, in other places vegan and vegetarian only. There are, however, hundreds of other shops, cafes, inns and hotels offering wholesome vegetarian dishes on their menus. We simply did not have the space to feature them all. See *The International Vegetarian Guide* for further details.

The same applies to the listing of museums of varying descriptions. Wales is steeped in history and there are far more ancient monuments, historic houses and sites than we could mention, most of them of genuine interest rather than part of the blatant heritage machine.

As far as bookshops are concerned, in addition to those we mention, it is also fair to say that most W.H. Smith branches stock local books and have an environment section, but they are not listed.

# Useful organisations

It has not been possible to list all groups and associations throughout Wales in the text. Here is a list of organisations which can refer you to local groups.

**Celtica Cymru**, a celebration and understanding of Celtic tradition, can be contacted through the Wales Tourist Board, Brunel House, Fitzalan Road, Cardiff CF2 1UY.

**Civic Trust for Wales**, Room 4, Llandaf Court, Fairwater Road, Cardiff CF5 2LN.

**Conservation Volunteers**, Forest Farm Road, Whitchurch, Cardiff.

**Mid Wales Development**, Ladywell House, Newtown, Powys SY16 1JB.

**Council for the Protection of Rural Wales**, 31 High Street, Welshpool, Powys SY21 7SD.

**Countryside Commission**, Office for Wales, Ladywell House, Newtown, Powys.

**Friends of the Earth** – see regional sections.

**Greenpeace**, 31 Islington Green, London N1 8XF, and see regional sections.

**Institute For Complementary Medicine**, 21 Portland Place, London W1N 3AF has a register of practitioners in Wales.

**Ramblers Association in Wales**, Pantwood, Pant Lane, Marford, Wrecsam, Clwyd LL12 8SG.

**Royal Association for Disability and Rehabilitation (RADAR)**, 25 Mortimer Street, London W1N 8AB publishes information for the disabled, as do the Wales Council for the Disabled, the Wales Tourist Board and Holiday Care Service.

**Royal Society for Nature Conservation**, The Green, Wilham Park, Lincoln LN5 7JR – see regional sections for wildlife groups.

**Soil Association**, 86 Colston Street, Bristol BS1 5BB provides information and sells lists of organic growers in Wales.

**UK 2000**, 4th Floor, Empire House, Mount Stuart Square, Cardiff CF1 6DN.

**Tourism Concern**, 8 St Mary's Terrace, Ryton, Tyne and Wear NE40 3AL.

**Vegetarian Society**, Parkdale, Dunham Road, Altrincham, Cheshire WA14 4QG.

**Welsh Craft Council**, 20 Severn Street, Welshpool, Powys SY21 7AD.

**Woodcraft Folk**, a national youth voluntary organisation dedicated to international friendship and peace, and love of the outdoors; has a Wales officer based at The Maltings, East Tyndall Street, Cardiff CF1 5EA.

**Woodland Trust**, Autumn Park, Dysart Road, Grantham, Lincolnshire NG31 6LL. There are several community initiatives regarding their woodlands in Wales.

**Youth Hostels Association**, Trevelyan House, 8 St Stephens Hill, St Albans, Hertfordshire AL1 2DY.

# Further Reading

N. Chadwick, *The Celts* (Penguin).
*The Mabinogian*, translated by Gwyn Jones and Thomas Jones (Everyman).
H. Gruffudd and E. Jones, *Welsh Is Fun* (Lolfa).
G. Borrow, *Wild Wales* (Gallery).
*South and Mid Wales New Shell Guide* (Michael Joseph).
M.K. Stone, *Mid Wales Companion* (Anthony Nelson).
C. Macdonald, *The Visitor's Guide to North Wales and Snowdonia* (M.P.C. Hunter).

# The Green Traveller

Let's start by trying to have a clearer idea of what is meant by the word 'Green'. Until fairly recently, it was not a very flattering term. Green as in 'greenhorn' means naïve, inexperienced, easily duped. Not exactly the kind of traveller we want to be.

But Green increasingly has become a kind of shorthand for anything which is environmentally and ecologically acceptable, a word for things that are good for you and do not (generally) foul up the planet even more.

Green also has rather more specialised meanings, linking it to lifestyles and philosophies which do not always fit into mainstream British life and values. It is also the name of one of Europe's youngest and, many people would argue, most vital political forces, a network of parties whose members campaign for political office and which occasionally, even in Britain, score major successes in terms of electoral support. Even without any parliamentary seats as yet, the British Greens are most certainly helping to shape the new political agenda of the 1990s as longer-established parties fall over each other to steal the Green Party's increasingly attractive environmental clothes.

This book is not about Green Party ideas. For those interested, Jonathon Porritt's excellent book *Seeing Green* provides a good background to the growth of the Green movement in Britain, whilst John Button's highly readable bestseller *How to be Green* is an everyday, practical guide on how to put Green ideas into practice.

Nor do we see the word Green being in any way limited to the activities of the Green Party or their sympathisers. As Jonathon Porritt argues so eloquently, Green politics as such is only one, albeit important, method of establishing Green ideas, and indeed the more such ideas become mainstream the less need there will be for a separate Green Party. 'Greenness' is something beyond party politics and national boundaries, and is both political and personal, a way of seeing and responding to what many people believe to be the catastrophe facing the human race and the planet we inhabit.

# Green travel and tourism

Tourism can and does have a negative impact on the environment – pollution, congestion, erosion, exploitation, urbanisation, as beautiful environments are dominated by the needs of mass tourism. The pattern is a familiar one: the discovery of a beautiful area of 'unspoiled' countryside or old town by a small group of cognoscente, followed by developers and tour operators who quickly transform the virgin area into a fashionable resort, with massive infrastructure soon following – high rise development, new high capacity roads, car parks, airports, ski lifts, timeshare. Local culture and colour is quickly eroded as the visitors import their own lifestyles, be it fish and chips and English pubs or frankfurters and lager. Eventually concrete deserts and overloaded environments result in gross pollution of beaches and drinking water and even avalanches in the Alps as slopes denuded of trees for ski runs become highly unstable.

Too many Mediterranean and Alpine resorts are a tragic witness to the exploitation of unique environments by the tourism business sector. In the

Far East tourism has become another form of colonialism, with scarce local resources such as water supplies used to create the artificial standards of Western luxury hotels and subservient local communities forced into alien lifestyles at subsistence wages. Does tourism need to be like this?

So deeply worrying have such developments become that opposition to mass tourism has emerged from many quarters, most notably in the Alpine regions where local environment groups have been formed to fight developers in a kind of resistance movement. In the former Portuguese colony of Goa the desire among local community groups to protect areas of beach and woodland threatened by hotel developers ran so high that tourist coaches were pelted with rotten fish and their occupants encouraged to stay away rather than acquiesce in the destruction of local habitats and the loss of livelihood for local people.

Groups such as Tourism Concern in Britain and Tourismus mit Einsicht in Germany, Austria and Switzerland are among those campaigning not against tourism as such, but towards the kind of more responsible, sustainable and ecologically acceptable tourism which the Swiss have called 'soft' or 'gentle' as opposed to the more traditional 'hard' tourism of the mass tourism industry.

Gentle tourism is as much about local culture as local environment. It seeks not only to enhance the quality of experience for the traveller or tourist, but to ensure something is put back into the host community, not just payment for services, but a response to different lifestyles and cultures which respects and even helps to enhance them.

Tourism will always be an intrusion. Indeed there are those who argue that gentle tourism is ultimately more intrusive and damaging than hard tourism, because if the tourists are contained in holiday centres or theme parks and have no contact with local communities they will intrude less on the lives of local people.

Such an argument seems to us to be defeatist. Many rural, particularly upland, areas of Europe – and Wales is no exception – are no longer economically self-sufficient and their communities seek a standard of living that even the Greenest of us regard as acceptable in the late twentieth century. Tourism is a method by which wealth can be re-distributed into these communities, providing support for local businesses and services, even for local production of foods, to enable them to survive and prosper.

Tourism can give small farmers a desperately needed second income to help them remain on the farm. Visitors can help small craft workshops and organic farms to survive. Visitors can help finance nature reserves, woodland management schemes, public transport, a local museum or heritage centre. Tourism can also help justify expenditure on environmental conservation and be a reason against its degradation and exploitation, whether by modern agribusiness, monoculture afforestation or insensitive industrialisation. Keeping countryside well managed and beautiful does not just benefit

7

visitors, but people who live there too, and pride in local heritage and culture is often only achieved when other people come along to share it and help to record or celebrate its happening.

Such positive examples of tourism – small-scale, locally controlled, environmentally responsible and culturally supportive – are what is now being described by such thinkers as Jos Krippendorf in Switzerland and Hans Heide in Austria as 'The New Tourism'.

The key to new tourism is local control. Local people through their democratic institutions, including voluntary bodies, need to have their say and ensure that what happens is what local people want to see, and not what is dictated by outside institutions and corporations, least of all foreign tour operators, airlines and coach firms, estate agents and developers. A prime example of this is the proposed development of a 'Quaritorium' in Llanberis, which could include a partly glazed roof covering a stage set on a lake, lasers, holograms, fabricated waterfalls and tropical vegetation. Alongside this there could possibly be, according to proposals, a hotel, conference facilities, restaurants, seven dry ski slopes and two toboggan runs. There have also been plans for holiday accommodation and a major housing estate. Local concern at the prospect of development out of context with the locality has led to the establishment of a local group, Padarn, which feels that if the proposals were implemented Llanberis would be overwhelmed.

As we have implied, tourism can be either a beneficial or a destructive activity. The Green traveller only travels and behaves in ways which have minimum negative impact on the environment. These will include ways of using his or her spending power, and tourism is certainly about spending money, to encourage positive tourist activity which benefits the community, directly or indirectly, in other ways. The slogan 'Think globally – act locally' is a good and practical guideline.

Cash for services will help the Welsh economy, whether the money goes to accommodation providers, cafes and restaurants, owners of environmentally sustainable attractions in town or countryside, local manufacturers of farm produce or artefacts, or operators of public transport and cycle hire. Tourism is partly about the creation of jobs and circulating money in the local economy, preferably not in the pockets of multinational hotel companies and leisure corporations, but in the hands of Welsh-owned enterprises whether country hotel or guesthouse, farmhouse, camp site or country inn, bookshop or publisher, woollen mill or candlemaker.

But Green travelling is not just about handing over cash and the creation of employment. It also depends on a real understanding of and respect for a unique European culture. You need to probe sometimes well beneath the surface and get off the beaten track to find the old, true, real Wales or even, on a different note, the emerging new Green Wales.

In Green travel terms, to paraphrase Schumacher, slow is beautiful. Green travelling is not about driving through Wales as fast as possible. It is not about driving at all. It is about planning and making journeys which may take a little longer – on foot, on a cycle, by country bus, by rural branch line railway – a journey in which travelling, which includes seeing and experiencing, is as important as getting there.

So the Green traveller must come to Wales prepared, albeit superficially, for his or her visit. It will require some reading and research to enrich the visit, not just tourist brochures with a hint of promotional hype, but local and national guides written as much for love of the country as for money. In fact it will require many visits, none to be rushed, to really begin to understand just some of the many subtleties and complexities, the mysteries, the contradictions, that are an essential part of the real Wales.

Don't expect this little Green Guide to do it all for you. All we can do is offer a few signposts, a few waymarks along the paths to be explored. The journey is yours to make – the delight as much in the planning as the execution.

# Green Wales

Wales is a remarkably Green land in more ways than one.

High rainfall and its peculiar geography make Wales literally one of the greenest lands in Europe – the soft greens of pastures, mountain sides, valley bottoms, forests, woodlands, lichens, mosses, bogs. Mild winters and relatively cool summers mean that the parched late summer landscapes of Central Europe or even Eastern England are relatively unknown.

But Wales is Green in other senses too. For one thing it does not have quite the population densities and consequent environmental pressures of many other Western European countries. Its 4,783,326 acres – about one-seventh the size of England – have a population of only 2.8 million, much of which is concentrated in the areas around Cardiff, Newport and Swansea in the south-east and along the coastal resorts of the north-east. This compares with a population of around 45 million for England, making Wales far less densely populated than its eastern neighbour. Most of the country is rural, and deeply rural in the sense of not being the kind of commuter or dormitory village countryside so prevalent in the English South-East and Midlands, though second and holiday home ownership is growing, a cause of concern for those seeking a decent housing stock for local people.

It is also a country where Green concepts have always been strong, either because they reflect traditional ways of life and husbandry which have not been destroyed by factory farming and agribusiness, or because Wales has been able to encourage, and indeed welcome, people who have followed alternative lifestyles of various kinds. Organic farming and wholefood shops and restaurants are on the increase in most parts of Wales.

The Wales Tourist Board has been among the leaders not only in the UK but in Europe in promoting Green tourism in varying ways, including the energetic promotion of farm-based holidays, walking and cycling holidays, craft centres, and strong support for public transport. Two initiatives illustrate how Wales is becoming perhaps a European leader in 'Green' education and tourism issues. Both are highly imaginative schemes with implications that go well beyond the boundaries of Mid Wales – the Mid Wales Festival of the Countryside and the Centre for Alternative Technology.

# Mid Wales Festival of the Countryside

This is a highly imaginative promotion by the Mid Wales Development Agency and the Countryside Commission for Wales under the patronage of Dr David Bellamy.

'Festival' is used in the sense of celebration, and this is built around the production each year of a Festival Brochure covering an area extending from southern Snowdonia, Montgomeryshire and the Borders, to the Brecon Beacons, the Teifi Valley and Cardigan Bay. The brochure lists countless small-scale rural attractions and country events, acting as a combination of a gazetteer and a diary of all that is available to the visitor and happening in this part of Wales during the summer months. Significantly, almost all the attractions shown have public transport information included. There is also an accommodation brochure to accompany the festival information.

Much of the thinking behind the Mid Wales Festival of the Countryside is economic, using Green tourism initiatives as a means of helping to support and revive the rural economy of central Wales, but it also encourages local people and visitors to spend time together.

The festival also reflects an important Welsh conservation strategy known as Cynefin, a word impossible to translate adequately into English, but meaning a sense of place, of belonging, of being at home and of 'rightness'.

The highly appropriate symbol for the Festival of the Countryside is the delicate yellow Welsh poppy, wild, free-flowering and in bloom during the time the festival takes place each summer.

# Centre for Alternative Technology

Mid Wales is also the setting for the Centre for Alternative Technology near Machynlleth. The Centre was founded in 1973 by Gerard Morgan-Grenville in order to demonstrate how people can live in ways which are less damaging to their environment and to the rest of the world's population. A charity was established, and a 40-acre disused slate quarry in the Dulas valley was chosen as the Centre's base. Work soon commenced to convert the derelict buildings to staff accommodation and exhibition areas with the aim of creating within Wales a truly sustainable lifestyle through environmentally responsible technology. The Centre opened to the public in 1976, following further help from charitable trusts and the Wales Tourist Board.

It is now a remarkable visitor and educational centre which uses wind and water power and solar energy for its own requirements. There is a wide range of organic gardens and allotments, using recycled waste products and sewage to produce humus-rich soils, and in greenhouses such as the inexpensive 'community polytunnel' there are many varieties of vegetables, fruit and flowering plants. There is an energy-saving insulated house which can operate on a fraction of the energy required for a conventional dwelling, therefore reducing not only costs but also the harmful effects of energy production. An excellent wholefood restaurant, a bookshop, a lecture theatre and accommodation have been added to the exhibition areas.

The Centre is not concerned with nostalgic throwbacks to the past or bogus heritage, though some tried and tested mechanisms such as windmills, waterwheels and ram pumps are to be seen. What the Centre is really all about is a vision of the future, when market forces have finally been allowed to squander our precious oil supplies and humanity is forced to find new, non-nuclear ways of surviving. Many of the energy-saving machines and techniques demonstrated on the site can be freely copied, with plans and drawings for sale in the shop, underlining the point that the prime purpose is to spread knowledge and often radical new ideas about sustainable technologies. There is even a commercial engineering branch of the Centre – Dulas Engineering Ltd. – capable of building energy-saving equipment and using intermediate technology for both the UK and the Third World.

A trail around the beautiful wooded site explains each technique and its purpose with clarity and often humour. Underlying the exhibitions is a deep philosophical awareness of humanity's responsibility for an increasingly threatened and vulnerable Earth, and the need to seek positive, humanitarian and above all practical solutions. The relative peacefulness of the site is itself a revelation.

More than 50,000 visitors each year come to experience the explicit, and more significant, the implicit messages of a place which has a special role in the European environmental movement. If the Green revolution has already begun to become a reality, you can watch it in action in a disused quarry in the centre of Wales. It is an experience not to be missed.

In the autumn of 1990, the Centre launched a £1,000,000 share issue to finance major expansion, including the building of a water-powered funicular. For details of this, together with further information about the Centre's activities, write to the Centre for Alternative Technology, Machynlleth, Powys SY20 9BR (0654) 702400.

# The landscape

An astonishing amount of the landscape in Wales is protected. There are no fewer than three National Parks – Snowdonia, the Brecon Beacons and the Pembrokeshire Coast – out of a total of eleven National Parks in England and Wales as a whole. Whilst not being 'national parks' in the UN definition of being nationally-owned and protected areas of land, they enjoy the highest level of landscape protection afforded in England to large areas of countryside.

There are also extensive areas of Welsh countryside enjoying the second level of landscape protection, in practice equally as rigorous. These are Areas of Outstanding Natural Beauty – such as those areas designated in Ynys Môn (Anglesey), the Clwydian Hills, the Llŷn Peninsula and the Wye Valley, whilst part of the Shropshire Hills area actually lies across the Welsh border in the county of Powys.

The Cambrian Mountains of Central Wales, once considered for national park status, now contain two large Environmentally Sensitive Areas. This is a relatively new form of designation which provides for direct assistance to the farming community to help conserve the landscape and protect natural beauty.

No part of Wales is far from the sea, and the country has an astonishing 750 miles of coastline. No fewer than fourteen individual stretches of this coastline, totalling approximately 495 miles and almost two thirds of the entire Welsh coast, are formally designated Heritage Coast, which means that they enjoy special landscape protection.

In addition there are a number of National Nature Reserves and Sites of Special Scientific Interest, which because of their value as habitats or for some special, perhaps geological feature, are of national interest and are given, in theory at least, rigorous protection.

Such an impressive list indicates how, in both British and European terms, the landscape of Wales is of exceptional beauty and interest. But bureaucratic lines on maps and officialdom are not what determines natural beauty. The landscape of Wales is the result of a complex interaction of natural and human forces over vast epochs.

## Geology, landscape and farming

Much is due to a particularly fascinating geology, which for centuries puzzled and baffled geologists and was only finally unravelled in the early nineteenth century by men such as Adam Sedgwick, who were able to explain the complex, shattered, twisted, contorted and eroded rocks that form the ancient peaks of Yr Eryri (Snowdonia). Not for nothing were the oldest sedimentary rocks known to Victorian science termed Cambrian, Ordovician and Silurian, named after ancient Welsh tribes by Sedgwick and his colleague, later rival, Murchison. Even more ancient, pre-Cambrian rocks are to be found in Ynys Môn (Anglesey) and on the Llŷn Peninsula, whilst both Pembroke and Yr Eryri (Snowdonia) have countless volcanic intrusions.

Rocks are the key to a landscape. In general terms, the older the rock, the harder it is, and the more it has withstood the erosive forces of wind, frost, rain, and ice to remain as jagged pinnacles or high ridges, rocky cliffs or mountain clusters. The ancient rocks of Wales are akin to those of the Lake District and parts of the Scottish Highlands and the landscapes have much in common. The erosive and scouring effects of glaciers are still clearly visible along the steep-sided valleys of Yr Eryri (Snowdonia), down which white waterfalls tumble into lakes trapped in the valley behind moraines of clay and debris left by the retreating ice. Such are the ingredients of all great romantic landscapes, from the Alps westwards, where the elements seem to be in perpetual conflict and dramatic moods predominate.

If you look at a relief map of Wales, it will be immediately evident how much of the land is over 200 metres – just over 600 feet – above sea level, which makes it officially upland, or indeed how much lies over 300 metres – 1,000 feet. These hills are the key to understanding Wales and it is a complex picture. In the north-east, leading from the Dee Estuary, are the Clwydian Hills which lead naturally into the Berwyns. These form an effective barrier before the high mountain ranges of Yr Eryri (Snowdonia) to the west, the peaks which culminate in the summit of Yr Wyddfa Fawr (Snowdon), at 3,560 feet or 1,085 metres the highest point in England or Wales. The foothills go to the coast and even extend out into the Llŷn Peninsula to the shores of the Irish Sea.

The great backbone of Wales is formed by the Cambrian mountains which run in a vast crescent from Yr Eryri (Snowdonia) down to the Teifi Valley and to the Preseli hills ending in a coastline of incredible beauty and richness, with offshore islands that are now internationally important bird sanctuaries.

To the east along the Marches lie the hills of Radnor Forest and the Black Mountains that with the River Wye form the Herefordshire border, then the Brecon Beacons, those superb great dome-like mountains which south of Merthyr Tydfil yield to the magnificent grassy ridges which separate the South Wales valleys, overlooking the Vale of Glamorgan and the Bristol Channel.

All these ranges are penetrated by deep valleys, almost inevitably filled with a swift-flowing mountain river difficult or impossible for navigation, sometimes following and deepening the channels caused by ancient glaciers.

It is easy to understand why such hills proved so hostile for settlement and so difficult and impenetrable for invading forces over centuries, why the Celtic peoples of Roman Britain were able to escape the invading Teutonic hordes of Saxons and Danes and why it was possible for the Welsh partisans to defend themselves so effectively against their English foes in the Middle Ages.

Travel was always difficult. Narrow mountain passes were arduous to cross on foot or horseback and always hazardous, while roads were difficult and expensive to build. Even the Industrial Revolution saw few canals except around the fringes and, in the heartlands, relatively few railways. Coastal shipping from such natural ports as Cardiff or Milford Haven was usually the easier option.

Mountain pastures have thin soils. Even the coastal strips near the mountainous areas are often rocky and narrow, and a cool, wet climate never turned Wales, with the possible exception of Ynys Môn (Anglesey) and parts of Pembrokeshire, into the kind of bread basket with rich cornfields such as those in the drier and flatter eastern part of England and even in Scotland.

So the rural economy of Wales was on the one hand largely a pastoral economy dependent on cattle and sheep, yet on the other hand mountains gave certain economic advantages, such as the existence of fast-flowing streams which were to provide abundant water power for driving corn and later textile mills in the early years of the Industrial Revolution.

As in England, the coming of the Normans into at least the less mountainous parts of Wales led to vast tracts of land being given to the monasteries. No fewer than seventeen Cistercian houses were established in Wales during the Middle Ages, many of them taking over, through their Norman patrons, older Celtic religious communities. The Cistercians in particular were highly capable farmers, clearing the forest, establishing extensive sheep walks and cattle farms from a system of outlying granges. This laid the foundation for the pastoral economy which continued well after the Dissolution.

The impact on the landscape of sheep and cattle farming has been the development of the traditional small hedge or stone wall enclosures in the valleys, and more extensive tree-less sheep walks on the open fell and mountainsides. In the eighteenth century, Welsh cattle were taken in large numbers to the great markets of the English Midlands and to London, and ancient drove roads can still be traced for miles across the desolate moorlands of Central Wales.

# Textiles and minerals

The monks also laid the foundation of the Welsh textile industry. Sheep wool was the raw material for both a wool and a flannel industry. This was followed by the spinning and weaving of cotton, particularly suited to the damp Welsh climate. Towns such as Ruthin and Dinbych (Denbigh) in Clwyd, Newtown and Llanidloes in Powys and villages along the Teifi Valley in Dyfed, where there was fast-flowing water to power mills, expanded as the new industry flourished. They were not able to meet the challenge of the huge new mills served by railways and canals in the highly industrialised towns and cities of the West Riding and Lancashire in Victorian times, and gradually declined in importance.

But the ancient rocks of the mountains were rich in other treasures – minerals. Copper and lead were to be found in hills in north and central Wales and even a little, much sought after, gold around the Mawddach Estuary west of Dolgellau and near Dolaucothi, Dinefwr. Silver as well as lead was mined around the Rheidol Valley inland from Aberystwyth.

The minerals which were to have the greatest impact on the landscape of Wales were slate, coal and iron. Slate is a form of mudstone, hard, ancient – mainly Silurian in origin – and fine grained, allowing it to be split cleanly and neatly. Vast quantities of slate were mined and quarried around Blaenau Ffestiniog in the nineteenth and early years of the twentieth century, and transported by narrow gauge steam railway down to the port of Porthmadog, to be shipped not only to parts of England but throughout the world. Many a fine roof is still covered with dark grey Ffestiniog slate. But it has left an almost lunar landscape of vast slate spoil tips around Blaenau Ffestiniog town. Equally immense quarries, now deserted, are to be found around Penrhyn and Dinorwic quarries, south of Bangor, from where slate was carried by rail to be shipped from Port Dinorwic.

The carboniferous rocks which cover the north-east and the south-east corner of Wales are, as their name implies, coal-bearing rocks, and it was the free-burning Welsh steam coal which for more than a century became synonymous with British industrial might. It fired the emblems of Britain's imperial power – transatlantic liners, Royal Navy frigates, Great Western express trains, as well as the nonstop mill wheels and furnaces of Victorian industry. Cardiff's growth and pre-eminence as a port grew from its vast coal exports in the period immediately before the First World War.

The happy coincidence in South Wales of vast quantities of ironstone close to seemingly inexhaustible coal seams led to the dramatic growth of Merthyr Tydfil, Llanelli, Port Talbot and other towns as part of one of the great iron and steel making centres of Europe, whilst Swansea became an important centre of the copper industry, eventually importing and processing huge quantities of Cornish copper ore, as did Llanelli with tin.

These industries developed, flourished and, in common with many other traditional European smoke-stack industries, eventually suffered decline

15

through a combination of cheap oil, coal imports, dwindling seams, rising costs, and foreign competition. This has left a blighted industrial landscape which only now is beginning to recover and to return to a green and wooded state as nature recolonises old workings and spoil tips, in some cases helped by imaginative conservation and restoration schemes. The greening of industrial South Wales over the last few years has been one of the most remarkable success stories of recent times. The view of the South Wales Valleys as being a blighted industrial wasteland is no longer true as spectacularly lovely landscapes re-emerge.

## Water and forestry

The impact of water reservoirs and forestry has been greatly underestimated in Wales. The building, at the beginning of the twentieth century, of the series of great reservoirs in and around the Elan Valley in central Wales resulted in the drowning of eighteen farmhouses, a school and a church, just to provide the city of Birmingham with badly needed water supplies – over 75 million gallons of water each day. The building of such reservoirs throughout rural Wales has continued, with loss of local farmland.

Forestry, in many respects, has become of even greater concern. Too much of Central Wales has been lost under the green tide of monoculture sitka spruce afforestation, undertaken both by the Forestry Commission and by private forestry syndicates. Afforestation presents a complex issue for conservationists. On the one hand Britain desperately needs more trees to help combat the greenhouse effect, and on the other hand single species plantations of conifers are not only drab in appearance, destroying the open feel of a landscape and choking out any undergrowth and much wildlife, but can add to the acidification of the soil which leads to increasingly acid run-off into lakes and streams. Experience has also shown that closely-planted, shallow-rooted conifers are highly vulnerable to storm damage, when large sections of woodlands can collapse in a domino or knock-on effect, and to acid rain. Mixed woodlands with sufficient native broad-leaved species may be less 'economic' in the short term, but produce a much more stable eco-system, particularly if trees of different ages are allowed to flourish and timber is taken out in small quantities rather than through periodic clear-felling. Hardwoods may have a greater long-term value than softwoods, which can be grown more cheaply and without subsidy or tax relief in areas like Scandinavia. The age-old technique of coppicing, for example, can produce valuable timber over a long period, whilst allowing wildflowers and a variety of bird and animal life to flourish in woodlands where air and light can penetrate.

16

## Hope for the future

To be fair, both the Forestry Commission and the private forestry syndicates are much more amenity-conscious than they were even a decade ago, and new hillside planting schemes no longer suffer from the harsh geometric outlines of older plantations, with some hardwoods and native species being included in most new schemes, particularly around the fringes. There is now a Forestry Commission broad-leaf planting scheme. Policies on public access are also very much better than they were in the past.

Let's hope that there is a continuing development of more environmentally acceptable and environmentally sustainable forms of woodland planting and management, such as the kind of small-scale woodland schemes increasingly being encouraged by the Countryside Commission for Wales and other conservation bodies. Over the next few years, these could make a remarkable difference to the landscape.

What would be particularly appropriate in Wales would be the kind of mixed farming and small-scale afforestation schemes which are so common in Austria and Germany. Farmers would receive woodland planting grants for approved species of trees, thereby providing shelter belts and, in future years, renewable sources of timber which could bring welcome additions to farm income. Such schemes would help to support farm enterprise and improve the landscape, reversing decades of officially encouraged neglect. Lack of attention to woodland maintenance, including walls and fences to keep livestock out, and methods to maximise production at the expense of the conservation of the countryside, have helped to degrade even the sublimely beautiful Welsh countryside. The Environmentally Sensitive Area experiment in the Cambrian Mountains could encourage new methods of conserving and even improving the landscape, whilst helping the farmer to earn an adequate return.

It is only through such a partnership with the Welsh farming community that this unique landscape will remain to delight this and future generations.

Serious consideration is also being given to at least one major new Community Forest in South Wales, a joint initiative to be undertaken by the Countryside Commission and other agencies. This would also make a tremendous difference to the beauty and variety of the urban landscape.

# The people and their history

Wales is a nation. It certainly is not, as many English people sometimes seem to tacitly assume, a crescent shaped chunk of England with a few mountains

17

and a rather nice coastline, attached to the West Midlands, where people speak with a funny accent.

It is one of the constituent nations of the United Kingdom, a proud, ancient land which too often loses its identity under that entirely artificial, largely eighteenth and nineteenth century notion of Britain which is, in reality, synonymous with England and English interests, in particular those of England's most prosperous south-east corner.

Maybe it is high time we began to ask what exactly we mean by Britain and Britishness, with its imperialistic overtones. Strictly speaking the only true Britons include the Welsh and the Cornish, who were occupants of these islands long before even the Romans came, let alone later generations of Angles, Saxons, Vikings and Normans. The truth about the United Kingdom is that it contains a richly varied community of peoples of different origins and backgrounds, traditions and expectations that are not easily classified by any term, least of all the word British.

Federalism, which is one of the fundamental democratic principles of many other European countries such as Austria, Germany and Switzerland, is a Green issue, because only when Wales is allowed to enjoy some degree of self-government within a wider United Kingdom federation and perhaps even a federal Europe will the domination of the 2.8 million Welsh by the 45 million English come to an end, and with it the ebbing of a cultural tide that threatens Wales' unique identity. But this is not merely a Welsh problem, as people in Scotland and for that matter the English regions will testify.

Wales has had a long and continuing struggle to retain its identity ever since the Celtic peoples of Britain, the Cymry as they called themselves (meaning comrades), were forced westwards from the lush lowlands of Shropshire and Herefordshire into the hostile mountains of what is now Wales by successive generations of Germanic invaders. They were described as 'Welsh' (meaning foreigners) by the pushy Saxons, eventually to find themselves contained behind a great earthwork, a boundary marker up to 18 metres high with a $3^{1}/_{2}$ metre wide ditch on the Welsh side. This was built in the eighth century by King Offa of Mercia and has ever since been known as Offa's Dyke.

The Norman Conquest was not particularly good news for either the English or the Welsh. Throughout late Norman and Plantagenet times not only were the more accessible and fertile parts of Wales handed over to the conqueror's acolytes – with such castles as Pembroke, Carew, Haverford-west, and Caerfilli – to dominate the native peoples by force of arms, but a system of 'marches' was operated to deal with often hotly disputed border-lands with England. Warlords, the Lords of the Marches, were given freedom to plunder deep into Welsh territory, in return for containing the Welsh, which they did from a line of castles and fortresses along the eastern border and through Cheshire, Clwyd, Powys, Shropshire, Herefordshire, Gloucestershire and Gwent.

A remarkable record of this period has survived in the form of chronicles written by a gifted Welsh cleric and monk, Giraldus Cambrensis (Gerald of Wales) who was born at Manorbier near Tenby and who eventually became Bishop of St. David's. His *Itinerarium* of 1188, written in Latin, provides a fascinating account of his journey around medieval Wales with Baldwin, Archbishop of Canterbury, visiting various castles and abbeys in order to drum up support among the Norman nobility for the Third Crusade. The *Itinerary of Wales* is available in modern translation.

But the Welsh heartlands remained under Welsh control and it was through the activities of two remarkable Welsh princes, Llywelyn ap Iorwerth and his grandson Llywelyn ap Gruffydd that Wales was able, in the thirteenth century, to reassert her identity. The first Llywelyn, often known as Llywelyn the Great, created an independent state of Gwynedd – the name used by the modern county – over much of North Wales. A Council of Welsh Princes was established at Aberdyfi, and Llywelyn even had time to take an interest in English affairs by supporting the English barons who imposed the Magna Carta on King John and by marrying Joan, John's illegitimate daughter.

The disputes and civil war which occurred after the death of Llywelyn the Great were only resolved with the emergence of his grandson, Llywelyn ap Gruffydd, who became such a powerful political leader that England's Henry III was forced, in 1276, to acknowledge him as the Prince of Wales, a title which continues to the present.

Llywelyn went on to take Welsh independence a stage further, finally rejecting all allegiance to the English crown and heading a united, independent Wales. But this act of defiance was to face the opposition of a much more formidable opponent, King Edward I. After Llywelyn was eventually slain at Builth in 1282, Edward completed his conquest by building a chain of massive castles at strategic points around the country – at Beaumaris, Conwy, Harlech, Rhuddlan, Flint, Denbigh and at Caernarfon. It was at Caernarfon that the future Edward II was enthroned as Prince of Wales in 1301. The tradition of investing the eldest son of the English monarch Prince of Wales at Caernarfon has continued ever since.

There followed a long period of anglicisation, with the English establishing new Saxon-style boroughs around their castles where the Welsh were excluded from holding land, trading or enjoying civil rights, reducing their status to that of a conquered or colonial people. Yet away from the official centres of power and administration, Welsh life and culture continued to flourish; most particularly there was a flowering of Welsh literature and poetry in the ancient oral tradition, led by bards attached to the old families.

Perhaps the greatest single piece of work to emerge from this period and to eventually find written form is the *Mabinogion*, a series of heroic romances, many of them with an Arthurian flavour, which are found in two important manuscripts, the *Book of Rhydderch* (written between 1300 and

1325) and the *Red Book of Hergest* (between 1375 and 1425), which together constitute a masterpiece of medieval European literature.

But a long period of economic hardship and increasing political oppression in the fifteenth century brought a period of unrest and the emergence of perhaps the most famous Welsh leader of all – Owain ap Gruffydd, better known as Owain Glyndŵr, anglicised to Owen Glendower, Shakespeare's enigmatic magician leader of the wild Welsh against the forces of King Henry IV.

A brilliant political leader as well as soldier, Glyndŵr united his country in rebellion, joining forces with dissident English nobles against the English monarchy, but despite establishing a Welsh Parliament in Machynlleth in 1404, he failed to get sufficient support to overthrow his powerful enemy. Nevertheless, Glyndŵr continued to wage a highly effective guerilla campaign against the English forces, and even though eventually defeated, he was never captured. His ultimate fate and death remain a mystery.

The results of these conflicts remain as tangible evidence in the landscape, most obviously in the series of castles, both English and Welsh, to be found in every almost part of the land.

When Henry Tudor, born in Pembroke and the grandson of one of Glyndŵr's kinsmen, Owen Tudor, became Henry VII of England after the Battle of Bosworth in 1485, it took some of the heat out of the Welsh struggle for independence. Henry Tudor soon brought 'emancipation and liberty' to his fellow countrymen, removing some of the harsh, almost racialist laws which had so incensed Glyndŵr and his followers. This process was continued by Henry Tudor's son Henry VIII, whose Secretary of State Thomas Cromwell created Acts of Union in 1536 and 1543 that helped to defuse Welsh nationalism and bring in a long era of relative Anglo-Welsh harmony, peace and prosperity. Welsh culture survived in the hinterlands, and its literature flourished both through the work of great poets who created an important post-medieval tradition, and indeed through Anglo-Welsh writers who have added their own distinctive voice to the written and spoken English language.

## Music, poetry and language

The Welsh hwyll or love of rhetoric and way with words still distinguishes Welsh people the world over, and whatever one's views might be of such diverse political figures as Lloyd George or Nye Bevan they shared an ability to use English with the vigour and wit characteristic of their nation. And there have been some outstanding Welsh poets in English too, for example the enormously popular and enigmatic Dylan Thomas (1914-53) of Swansea, of *Under Milk Wood* fame, the fine Second World War poet Alun Lewis (1915-44), and that austere defender of Welsh nationhood and identity, R.S.

Thomas, who has been justly described as one of the greatest English-speaking poets of our time.

Centuries of intermingling of peoples have inevitably created a diversity of cultures that are all authentically and uniquely Welsh. The coming of Flemish weavers to Pembrokeshire, creating together with English immigrants a 'Little England beyond Wales', has added a flavour to West Wales which is different from the English-speaking industrial valleys of South Wales, many of whose inhabitants originated from the English Midlands. There has always been an Anglo-Welsh squirarchy throughout Wales which enjoyed such typically English pursuits as fox hunting rather more than fishing from a traditional coracle on the River Teifi, and which almost certainly identified more closely with its fashionable English cousins than its Welsh neighbours.

The industrialised areas of South Wales, especially the mining areas with their strong tradition of chapel-going, their love of great music and fine singing (Welsh choirs are equalled only by those of the West Riding), and rugby football, together with a deep respect for education, have their own strong, rich culture and sense of comradeship every bit as much as their northern cousins. Their influence has been felt worldwide, Richard Llewellyn's novel of the harsh times of the 1930s, *How Green Was My Valley*, provides a vivid record of life in the Rhondda among the mining communities.

Nor is it possible to ignore recent newcomers to Wales, mainly English people, coming to settle and be a permanent part of the community. Some come with illusions, some with ideals, some with the problems they have left behind in the crowded cities and suburbs of England. But others will have much to offer and many of the Green initiatives listed in these pages are originated by people who made a conscious choice to follow an alternative lifestyle in the Welsh countryside. Welsh cultural values are important. For it is really the Welsh-speaking Welsh, a minority in their own land as they have now become, that is the community that keeps alive a very special sense of Welsh identity and uniqueness, and for whom any further inroads into their linguistic heritage would be a great tragedy indeed.

Over the last century or so, with improved communications, and most particularly since the advent of the modern audio and visual media of radio, film and television, the Welsh language – Cymraeg – has had to fight a rearguard action.

One illustration of how much things have changed in Wales over the last century or so can be obtained from reading George Borrow's delightful book *Wild Wales*. In 1854 George Borrow undertook an extended walking tour mainly in North but also in Mid and South Wales, which eventually was to lead to his highly readable book. Whilst he described the landscape and antiquities seen on his travels, the real focal point of the book are the people Borrow met in inns and taverns or along the highway or footpath. This is

21

coupled with his extensive knowledge and love of Welsh literature, and the point of much of his travelling in Wales was to visit the birthplaces or graves of a number of great medieval Welsh writers, particularly such poets as Gronwy Owen or Dafydd Ap Gwilym, whom he describes as the Welsh Ovid. The significant point is that the vast majority of the people Borrow met were Welsh speakers. Borrow was himself, unusually for an Englishman, a fluent reader and speaker of Welsh, much to the astonishment of those he met. This ability was very necessary in the Wales of the 1850s, for many of the people he came across had not a word of English.

To an extent, Borrow was the perfect Green traveller, one who had acquainted himself thoroughly with the language and culture of his hosts, who was alive and awake with curiosity at everything he saw and everyone he met, and who made contact and friendships wherever he travelled. The picture he gives of Wales as it was in the middle of the last century is a fascinating one. Even to an energetic, experienced traveller like Borrow, parts of Wales were as remote as modern Peru would be to a contemporary writer.

Less than a century and a half later, the chances of a visitor meeting anyone in Wales unable to speak English are remote. Though Welsh – Cymraeg – remains the mother tongue for a sizeable community of people, mainly in Mid and North Wales, it is now a minority language within its own land. Only around 580,000 Welsh speakers remain, compared with about 650,000 twenty years ago, a rate of decline which suggests that without drastic action the tongue could be extinct well before the end of the next century.

The reasons for this decline are many and complex. Reputedly older than Ancient Greek, Welsh belongs to the Celtic peoples and is broadly similar to Breton, Earse, Gaelic and Cornish. Modern communications, ease of travel, radio and television have all provided a constant bombardment by the dominant Anglo-Saxon culture, which is proving as effective in eliminating the Welsh linguistic heritage as anything Edward's castles could provide. As young people leave for English cities to seek work, they leave their native language and culture behind them. Incomers, perhaps to retirement homes in the mountains or along the coast, are English speakers. The large new holiday resorts created by the railways in the last century also brought in not only thousands of visitors from nearby English conurbations, but hoteliers and entrepreneurs to service their needs and sharing an identical background. Even today you are as likely to hear the gutteral vowels of Oldham or Merseyside in Rhyl or Abergele, or of the Black Country in Abermaw (Barmouth), as a soft Welsh lilt.

Fortunately there has been effective resistance to the constant erosion, thanks to bodies like the Welsh Language Society and Plaid Cymru. The annual Eisteddfoddau have kept alive the traditions of Welsh poetry and music throughout Wales. Teaching of the language in schools and Welsh channels on radio and above all on television have together helped create a new awareness and real revival of interest. Welsh language is a strong political issue. There are signs that young people in particular increasingly value their heritage, with some evidence of a welcome increase in the number of Welsh speakers in recent years.

Plaid Cymru has become a powerful and effective political force in the northern half of Wales, with three Members of Parliament who have done much to advance the Welsh cause. This has proved much more effective than the burning of property and violence, a few headline-capturing examples of which by extremist groups have only served to fuel prejudice and damage the cause.

For there are enormously important reasons for keeping Welsh as a living language. Language is culture, two thousands years or more of the rich, complex, subtle history of a people. Once it is forgotten, removed from the lives of ordinary country people into the dusty mausoleums of libraries, learned societies and archives, reduced to mere (for the English) unpronounceable place names, a major part of our common European heritage would be dead and lost forever.

It must never be allowed to happen. The fluent music of the Welsh tongue in a bus, in a shop, on a street corner or in a pub, is as important as the unspoiled beauty of the mountainside and incomparable coastline and to share a little of it, even as an uncomprehending visitor, is a privilege. But for the Welsh people themselves its loss would be an immeasurable tragedy.

## FURTHER READING

A.H. Dodd, *A Short History of Wales* (Batsford).
Giraldus Cambrensis, *Itinerary* (Penguin Classics).
*The Mabinogion*, translated by Gwyn Jones and Thomas Jones (Everyman).
George Borrow, *Wild Wales* (Gallery Books).
Richard Llewellyn, *How Green Was My Valley* (Hodder).

# Getting around without a car

One area where many of us find ourselves in a situation of compromise is public and private transport. The car is just too convenient. Flexibility, freedom from timetables, the ability to go where and when you want are advantages which are too obvious to be emphasised. For many people a car is synonymous with personal freedom and public transport is something they use only occasionally.

Add to this government policies which tacitly or otherwise have encouraged the ownership and use of cars almost as a virtue, heavy promotion from the industry, and cheap energy policies which even after recent price increases leave car ownership and usage available to more people than ever before in our history – and if Britain was a group of tiny, underpopulated islands that might be the end of the story.

But it is not. More than twenty million cars on these islands, using up huge quantities of natural resources, causing enormous congestion and pollution and physical danger, now make motor transport probably the greatest single source of environmental degradation and pollution which our own and future generations have to suffer. Official Department of Transport figures predict a further doubling of the number of vehicles on our roads by the early decades of the next century and existing policy directives strive to achieve this. Such a figure, an environmental nightmare in itself, has alarming implications in terms of the already acute problems now being suffered. The warning signs have been there for some time: massive queues waiting to leave London at Bank Holiday times, Lake District roads being physically shut to stop more cars coming in during some summer days and the Peak District having to restrict cars in areas which cannot take any more. Wales has not been hit so hard, but it is coming. The Gower Peninsula, the roads to Tenby and increasing pressure on parts of Ynys Môn (Anglesey) and Yr Eryri (Snowdonia) should be sufficient warning.

But it will be some time before grim realities of congestion, pollution and shortages begin to affect the behaviour of the average UK motorist. Air pollution caused by road traffic, in small towns as much as big cities, is now reaching catastrophic proportions, the full scale of which is in many ways being concealed by the government's constant refusal to provide continual monitoring of the situation. Add to this the tolls of thousands of people killed and maimed each year, the no less relevant visual pollution by cars of town and countryside, and the fact that traffic noise is something that pervades even remoter and mountainous areas.

How long government transport policies can continue to fly against not only empirical evidence of the damage to the environment and to the mobility of people without cars, who form a majority if individuals rather than households are measured, but also against public opinion, remains an open question. Changes are likely to come as much through medical opinion as the environmental lobby.

Need it be like this?

Such issues are of deep relevance to Wales, where towns and cities are suffering the same acute congestion and pollution as the rest of Europe, and where public transport systems are suffering from the same kind of myopic policies by which essential funding is denied both for capital investment and revenue support. The situation is likely to get worse at the time of writing, with renewed risk of economic recession and the effects of Poll Tax making local authorities even less able to support loss-making rural public transport services from scarce and dwindling funds.

Over the last few decades there has been a progressive run-down of public transport, closure of railway lines and reduction of services in rural areas. Fares have also been allowed to rise far faster than the cost of living, and very much faster than the actual cost of motoring. Worst of all, and symptomatic of remote, privileged policy makers who regard use of public transport as a kind of 'Poor Law' provision to be provided at the lowest possible cost, has been the deregulation of the bus industry. This has directly led to a further reduction of services and loss of passengers in some areas, particularly during the evenings and on Sundays.

In this situation, even readers of a Green Guide might well be tempted to throw in the towel and determine that the only way Wales can be visited is by car.

But by so doing, you worsen the problem. In this book, we encourage you to leave your car and try other forms of transport – walking, cycling, bus and train. Despite the issues raised above there has been an increase in cycle provision and there is scope for a lot more. Furthermore, many local authorities in Wales such as Mid Glamorgan and Gwynedd have fought hard to keep a reasonable bus and train network together. Thus travel without the car is possible and if you aim to wean yourself off total car dependence gently there are considerable positive advantages.

Train and bus travel, from elevated seats looking over hedges and walls, offers far better views of the countryside than a low-slung car. Railways are rich with inherent interest. They are often feats of superb engineering and architectural heritage in their own right, full of history – particularly the Welsh standard and narrow gauge lines which often penetrate deep into the countryside away from crowded roads. Buses too find their way into the very heart of the countryside, serving small communities where tourists hardly go, and the fact that they are slower than cars means there is longer to absorb and savour the countryside. The country bus is a mobile meeting place, where in rural Wales you are likely to hear the driver switch with fluent ease between Welsh and English, to meet people shopping and about their daily business, to observe such delightful touches as a granddaughter meeting her grandmother on the market day bus and breaking into the kind of concerned gossip that only happens between generations.

With just a little trouble and forethought, it is in fact perfectly possible to get around most of Wales without a car, and we would contend that it is a far more rewarding and enjoyable way of experiencing the real life of the countryside.

Of course your journey will take longer and you have to plan ahead. Absolutely essential in the present conditions is to get hold of up-to-date timetables (all local authorities in Wales provide these – some are particularly efficient). There will be irritations and annoyances with services running late and awkward connections, sometimes involving long waits – though local cafes and pubs are often adequate compensation.

Naturally it will be more trouble. It will perhaps be very difficult if not impossible to get everywhere you might like to go. For some people, perhaps those with young children (though young children love trains and buses) or an elderly relative, or a disability, public transport might not be a realistic option. Some journeys simply do not work.

The fact also has to be faced that even with such civilised facilities as Student, Family and Senior Citizen Railcards and some excellent bus and rail rover tickets, the cost of getting around by public transport might still be unfavourable compared with the cost of four people in a small car, especially if the journey is a difficult cross-country one requiring changes of service and perhaps mode.

On the other hand, it is surprising how much can be done conveniently and pleasantly by bus and train, even if the occasional taxi has to be used (for example to get rid of the problem of dragging luggage behind you). Taxis are public transport too, and their use helps the local economy.

It comes down to a question of personal responsibility and doing what is possible. The research for this book was done travelling in Wales by bus, train and on foot, even into some quite remote corners, and hugely enjoyable it was too. Maybe it is a matter of using the car as little as possible, or as a last resort, and wherever practical and possible using public transport alternatives (which also helps safeguard such services for the local community); or not travelling great distances at all, but spending more time exploring the place you are in and getting to know it better on foot or by cycle. Whatever your stance, have a go at travelling the slower way for part if not all of your holiday.

First of all you need to understand the networks, which in spite of penny-pinching cuts are still very largely intact.

## Railways

Begin by looking at the British Rail network, which provides the basic longer distance public transport services in Wales and several important local services. For convenience the Welsh rail network might be grouped into three main areas – the North, Central Wales and the Borders, and South and West Wales.

North Wales has the coast line from Chester through the coastal resorts, with branches from Chester to Wrecsam and Shrewsbury, and from Llandudno Junction to Deganwy and Llandudno; the line continues to Bangor, across the Menai Bridge to Ynys Môn (Anglesey) and to Caergybi (Holyhead). This line carries InterCity services from London and the Midlands and fast direct Sprinter 'regional' services from Crewe and the Midlands and from both West Yorkshire and Greater Manchester.

At Llandudno Junction one of the most beautiful branch lines in Wales, the Conwy Valley Line, follows the Afon Conwy down to Llanrwst, Betws-y-Coed and Blaenau Ffestiniog where during the summer months it links with the superb little Ffestiniog narrow gauge steam railway to Porthmadog through the heart of Yr Eryri (Snowdonia).

The principal railway along the Welsh borders is the Marches Line which runs from Shrewsbury via Hereford, Ludlow, Abergavenny and Newport to Cardiff with through Sprinter trains from Manchester and Crewe. The Heart of Wales Line leaves this route at Craven Arms for a magnificent rail journey through some of the wildest and grandest scenery of Wales, past Knighton, Llandrindod Wells and Llandeilo to Llanelli and Swansea.

The Cambrian and Cambrian Coast Lines run from Shrewsbury to Machynlleth and Dovey Junction, one of the few stations in Britain without road access, from where the lines split; the Cambrian Line sweeping westwards around the Dyfi estuary to Aberystwyth, the superbly beautiful Cambrian Coast Line heading north to Aberdyfi, Tywyn, Abermaw, Harlech, Porthmadog and Pwllheli.

South Wales is primarily served by the InterCity main line from London Paddington via Bristol Parkway and the Severn Tunnel to Newport, Cardiff and Swansea, with some services supplemented by local connections continuing to Pembroke Dock, Haverfordwest, Milford Haven and Fishguard. But a particularly important local network is provided by the Valley Lines out of Cardiff into Taff Vale, the Rhondda and other former mining valleys.

The British Rail network is supplemented by 'The Great Little Trains of Wales', in essence tourist railways in the form of narrow gauge steam lines, though some of them, most notably the Ffestiniog Railway, also provide an important public transport service. The number of steam lines, including such delights as the Talyllyn Railway, the world's oldest preserved line, the Ffestiniog Railway itself with its unique spiral, the Vale of Rheidol, the Welshpool and Llanfair, the Bala Lake, the Llanberis Lake, the Fairbourne and Barmouth and the Brecon Mountain railways, and not forgetting the rack-and-pinion Snowdon Mountain Railway, make Wales one of the prime areas in Europe for the narrow gauge steam enthusiast.

A range of special tickets brings down the price of travelling through Wales by train. These include the seven-day Freedom of Wales Ticket which gives unlimited travel around the whole of the Welsh rail network including lines which cross the border to and from Chester, Shrewsbury and Hereford.

A less expensive North and Mid Wales Rover covering an area from Aberystwyth to Shrewsbury and Crewe has the added advantage of offering free travel on the Ffestiniog Railway, on almost all Crosville Wales (the principal operator) buses in the area, and on all buses in Gwynedd County, making it a superb ticket for the Green traveller in the northern part of Wales. Children and railcard holders get good discounts on both Rovers.

Rail Rover Tickets can be booked at principal stations and British Rail agents, and if booked in advance can be planned to coincide with part of an arrival journey in Wales. Overseas visitors can take advantage of the Brit Rail

Pass – which takes in the whole of the British Rail network including Wales and which can only be purchased through British Rail agencies in their own country – or Regional Rover tickets, whilst young people under 26 from overseas can use an Inter-Rail ticket on all the UK networks.

Towns such as Llandudno, Abermaw (Barmouth), Aberystwyth, Haverfordwest or even Cardiff are particularly well placed to exploit the opportunity of discovering much of Wales by rail with a Rover ticket. There are also a choice of Day Ranger and Evening Ranger tickets available for particular lines. Look out for local publicity.

## Buses

Buses provide an even greater degree of penetration into the countryside, as well as some of the strategic routes no longer provided by rail. These include routes in Central Wales from Haverfordwest to Aberystwyth, and from Caerfyrddin (Carmarthen) to Aberteifi (Cardigan). Particularly important for cross-Wales journeys are the Trawscambria coach service 701 from Cardiff and Swansea to Aberystwyth and Bangor and the Expresswest service 612 from Haverfordwest and Pembroke to Bristol.

The northern part of Wales is still dominated by Crosville Wales, the former National Bus Company subsidiary which provides the backbone of the area's services, including such scenically beautiful routes as service 94 from Wrecsam to Abermaw (Barmouth), service 2 from Aberystwyth to Bangor, services 562-8 from Aberystwyth around Plynlimon, and several services in Yr Eryri (Snowdonia). The company offer a superb value Crosville Rover day and weekly ticket over the whole of their network. Gwynedd County Council (whose information service and support for local bus services is particularly excellent) have a Bws Gwynedd Rover ticket priced for adults, children and families, valid anywhere in the County, making bus travel cheaper than the family car. To make the offer even more attractive, if you produce your Bws Gwynedd Rover ticket at a number of tourist attractions you can get up to 20% off admission charges – a real bonus for Green travellers. Gwynedd issue a regular series of timetable leaflets for each of their districts, plus a rail timetable.

Gwynedd County Council also supports the Snowdon Sherpa network through the heart of Parc Cenedlaethol Eryri (Snowdonia National Park), which is designed to reduce pressure from motor traffic on the Park. Services link with trains and a shuttle bus service operates between car parks in the Llanberis Pass.

Both Powys and Dyfed support a range of local services, including the Brecons Rambler bus linking with South Wales rail services and serving the heart of Brecon Beacons National Park.

The other particularly well bussed areas include South Wales, where National Welsh and its subsidiaries operate a network of services into the

Forest of Dean, the Brecon Beacons, the Vale of Glamorgan and the South Wales Valleys. South Wales Transport operate further west into Pembroke and the Gower Peninsula, which is well served by the company's service 18 bus from Swansea. Richards Brothers provide a good local network between Caerfyrddin (Carmarthen), Aberteifi (Cardigan) and Haverfordwest.

Not to be forgotten for a real 'Green travel' experience is the postbus network, of which no fewer than twelve services operate, mainly in Central Wales and the Marches, and which includes some extremely remote villages and communities. For details pick up the Royal Mail Postbus Guide (which includes detailed timetables) available from Post Offices or Tourist Information Centres throughout Wales or from Post Office Public Affairs, 30 St. James's Square, London SW1Y 4PX. They do not all run every day, and often leave at quite early hours, so careful planning may be required.

## Cycling and walking

Cycling is another superb way to discover Wales, and there are a number of firms offering special packages of cycle hire and accommodation. Cycle hire is an excellent way of getting to those places where buses do not run, and it is often a lot easier with present-day Sprinter and Pacer trains not to bring your bike with you by rail but to hire one when you arrive. It also means that you need not cycle every day, but perhaps just enjoy one or two days awheel. The Trans Cambrian Trail or Lonydd Glas Cymru should be coming to fruition during 1991 and what a marvellous route it is. Part cycleway, part tracks and back lanes, the trail runs from Caergybi (Holyhead) to Cardiff and Newport. Co-ordinated by the very adventurous Sustrans organisation, this will hopefully lead to a series of spurs and linked routes making Wales so much more attractive to the would-be cyclist who is rightly wary of main roads.

Local cycle hire facilities are included in the appropriate local sections.

Walking is, of course, another especially Green way of getting around, and few experiences compare with rambling a long-distance footpath or trail as a way of sensing the beauty and majesty of a landscape.

The most popular long-distance route in Wales is undoubtedly the 180-mile Pembrokeshire Coast Path between Aberteifi (Cardigan) and Kilgetty, followed by the 142-mile Offa's Dyke Path which, as its name implies, follows Offa's Dyke through the Welsh Marches. Both are National Trails. Other popular routes include the Powys and the Gwent Wye Valley Walks, the Usk Valley Walk, the Coed Morgannwg Way, the Taff Valley Trail, Glyndŵr's Way, the Dyfi Valley Walk, the Cambrian Way and the Maelor Way.

Specialist companies offering walking holidays are listed in the regional sections.

FURTHER INFORMATION

**British Rail:** Shrewsbury (0743) 64041; Llandudno Junction (0492) 585151; Swansea (0792) 467777.
**Ffestiniog Railway:** (0766) 512340/831654.
**County Council public transport enquiry lines:** Clwyd (0352) 2121; Dyfed (0267) 233333; Gwent (0633) 838838; Gwynedd (0286) 4121; Mid Glamorgan (0222) 820626; Powys (0597) 826643; South Glamorgan (0222) 499022; West Glamorgan (0792) 471232.

**Main bus operators:** Crosville Wales (0492) 596969; South Wales Transport (0792) 475511; National Welsh (0222) 371331; Richard Bros (0239) 613756. Doe's Bus/Rail Guide, produced by Travadvice, is a very useful book which details major bus links from railway stations. Phone (0202) 528707.

# Accommodation and food

Having solved the means of travelling around Wales, the problem remains of where to stay and what to eat.

## *Accommodation*

Accommodation is perhaps the simplest problem of all. There is no shortage of quite excellent accommodation throughout the whole of Wales, from campsites, youth hostels and simple bed-and-breakfast right through to luxurious country hotels and even, in the cities, luxury-class expense account business hotels that have little to do with Green travelling.

If you are able to make a choice, whenever possible take advantage of independent, locally-owned enterprises rather than national or even international chains, as this will help to ensure that money spent and profit earned stays in the locality rather than being paid into the pockets of distant shareholders.

An exception, of course, is the Youth Hostels Association (YHA), that dedicated voluntary organisation which over the past sixty years or so has helped to create so many opportunities for young people of limited means to enjoy the countryside. Whilst people with cars are allowed to use them, they are primarily aimed at walkers and cyclists and are often strategically situated with them in mind. Despite the name, there is no age restriction. There is a particularly excellent network of YHA hostels in Wales, which vary from a castle and grand, if faded, country houses down to simple farm buildings, a former school and even an old lifeboat house. Youth hostelling still remains one of the most economical and enjoyable ways of discovering Wales, and of meeting people in friendly and pleasant surroundings.

The Wales Tourist Board provides a quite superb range of information about all types of accommodation, and a telephone call to any of their offices (see below) is recommended. There is a strong emphasis on farmhouse accommodation, which is particularly Green in that it gives the visitor the chance not only to stay in the heartland of Wales away from the overused tourist areas, but to get close to the real life of the countryside, whilst at the same time making a useful contribution to farm incomes. There is a range of brochures outlining all types of accommodation on offer, ideas for short breaks or longer-stay holidays and a direct telephone booking service on (0792) 645555. The Wales Tourist Board also produces a series of guidebooks, costing around £3 each but excellent value, to Hotels and Guest Houses, Bed and Breakfast Accommodation, and Self Catering. Each also contains useful detailed maps. They can be obtained from any Tourist Information Centre in Wales or from one of the Wales Tourist Board offices listed below. There is also the free Welsh Festival of the Countryside accommodation guide, covering much of Mid Wales.

Whilst on the one hand it makes sense to ensure any accommodation you are booking is Wales Tourist Board registered, to ensure minimal standards, you also have to remember that operators usually have to pay to be included in the guide, which inevitably means that the glowing descriptions on the page are advertising hype rather than objective commentary. It pays to read between the lines and guess at what is not said – for example distances from railway stations or bus stops if you happen to be depending on public transport.

As in England, it is possible to camp anywhere in Wales if you have the landowner's, usually the farmer's, permission, but that permission can only be given for a very few days of the year without breaking planning regulations. You may prefer to use an officially registered site that will have proper washing and sanitation facilities.

Caravans and mobile homes, which are not in our view especially Green because of the congestion and visual intrusion they cause, can only be parked on an officially approved site. Overnight parking, for example in a car park or lay-by, can be a criminal offence and result in prosecution.

Slightly more difficult is the question of static caravans which, unless they are well screened, can be a blight on the countryside. Wales, as almost everywhere else in Britain, has parts of its coastline disfigured by hideous lines of pale-coloured vans which are often quite appallingly intrusive. There is also less economic benefit to the locality if, as sometimes happens, caravanners arrive by car with a box of groceries from their local super-market rather than spending money in local shops.

On the other hand, a caravan holiday is often the only kind of holiday which many people can enjoy in the countryside and this has to be recognised. The answer is perhaps to ensure that existing sites are improved and better screened and that new sites, particularly in hitherto unspoiled areas, are resisted.

## FURTHER INFORMATION

**Wales Tourist Board offices:**
Head Office, 12th Floor, Brunel House, 2 Fitzalan Road, Cardiff CF2 1UY.
Wales Centre in London, 34 Piccadilly, London W1V 9PB (071) 409 0969.
South Wales Regional Office, Tŷ Penfro, Charter Court, Phoenix Way, Enterprise Park, Swansea (0792) 781212.
Mid-Wales Regional Office, Canolfan Owain Glyndŵr, Machynlleth, Powys SY20 8EE (0654) 702401.
North Regional Office, 77 Conway Road, Colwyn Bay, Clwyd LL29 7LN (0492) 531731.

Local **Tourist Information Centres** are listed in the appropriate regional sections of this book.

**The Festival of the Countryside (Mid Wales)**, Frolic Street, Newtown, Powys SY16 1AP (0686) 625384.

## Food

Most non-Welsh people associate Wales with only one vegetable, that highly underrated culinary delight the humble leek, sported with such pride at international rugby matches. But there is far more to Welsh food than leeks or laverbread (made from edible seaweed).

As Gilli Davis argues in an informative essay in *A Taste of Wales*, the Romans were already fishing the rivers for salmon and gathering oysters and cockles from the beaches and planting vineyards in Gwent and Glamorgan. They were distilling Welsh whisky on Ynys Enlli (Bardsey Island) as early as the fourth century and the Vikings were finding edible seaweed around Solva in Pembrokeshire.

A strong Celtic influence remained in Welsh country food right until the present century, with an emphasis on nourishing meat (pork or lamb), vegetable stews and oat bakestone cakes cooked on the farmhouse griddle. There was always an abundance of milk, with farmhouse butter and cheeses in good supply, and there would be hams curing in the kitchen and bottled fruit in the pantry.

One of the very positive aspects of tourism in recent years has been a strong revival of interest in traditional food and recipes, leaving behind the kind of fast food to be found across the globe.

There are, for instance, no less than sixty kinds of delicious Welsh farmhouse cheeses, of which Caerphilly is only the most famous. Goats' cheese is now manufactured around Abergavenny (it was the most common cheese in Wales until the eighteenth century), whilst there has been a revival of interest in traditional breadmaking, and in cakes and pastries.

One typically Welsh favourite, found almost everywhere in Wales, and served with tea, is bara brith, which means speckled bread and is a fruit loaf best made with wholemeal flour.

Welsh lamb already enjoys an international reputation and can be cooked in very much more exciting ways than as just a roast with green peas. There is also a revival of interest in fish dishes, particularly salmon, trout and crab, and in the use of herbs.

So seriously do the Welsh take the interest in well-produced, locally grown food that a Wales Tourist Board sponsored project known as 'Taste of Wales' exists to promote good quality Welsh food, including recommended pubs, hotels and restaurants serving it. The book of the same name, *A Taste of Wales*, puts Welsh food in context and provides a guide to what is a very exciting culinary scene, with an emphasis on healthy eating.

Organic farming is traditional in Wales although not many farms remain pure. Organic restaurants and wholefood shops are on the increase. The Green traveller will almost certainly be able to find excellent wholefood and vegetarian restaurants and bistros in most of the towns and even larger villages. We list some of these in the regional sections of this book.

## Wine and beer

Nor is it just a question of the production of real food in Wales. Welsh vineyards are once again in operation, and Welsh vintages are produced near Monmouth, at Llantrisant and in the Vale of Glamorgan, whilst a mellow Welsh whisky comes from Dafydd Gittins' distillery at Brecon.

For those who enjoy real ale, there is a plentiful supply of outlets of cask-conditioned beer, but not much is brewed in Wales. In North Wales the supply comes mainly from North-West England, although no one seems to grumble too much about that. In Mid Wales Banks, a fine brew from the Midlands, is well represented. What of locally brewed ale? Plassey near Wrecsam produce a fine pint of Farmhouse Bitter and in Mid Wales Sam Powell is brewed in Newtown. In the borderlands, two English beers are shipped in, Woods from Shropshire and Wye Valley from Hereford, both superb offerings. Herefordshire also provides pubs with some real ciders such as Dunkertons and Westons, rather than the keg brands, but they are not found often.

It is to South Wales that we look for authentic Welsh brews. Pembrokeshire Own Ales from Llanteglos brewery near Amroth has a strong local following. Llanelli is still a brewing town of distinction with Felinfoel and Buckley ales extremely popular. The former is as independently minded as a small brewery can be these days, but Buckley belongs to one of the larger combines as do most of the other brews sold in these parts. The exception is Brains brewery in Cardiff, a very traditional affair, selling a brew to whet the taste of any thirsty soul. The Raisdale Hotel in Penarth also brews real ale on the premises for its guests.

The Campaign for Real Ale (CAMRA) has recently begun a regional series of books published by Alma Publications, of which Mike Dunn has written one about beer in North Wales, and branches of CAMRA usually publish local leaflets or booklets with information about local breweries and hostelries which tend to be sold in local bookshops and pubs. May the tradition of small-scale breweries continue against an increasing tide of international or national brewing of keg products.

## FURTHER READING

Richard Binns, Gilli Davies and Brenda Parry, *A Taste of Wales* (A Taste of Wales, Wales Tourist Board joint publication).
David Mabey and Alan and Jackie Gear, eds., *Thorsons Organic Consumer Guide* (Thorsons).

# PART 2
# THE REGIONS
# OF WALES

# Ynys Môn – The Isle of Anglesey

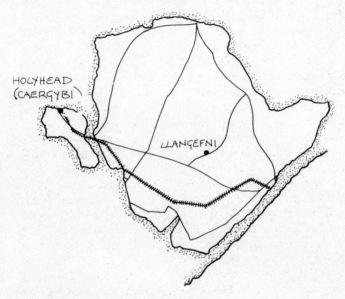

The old saying 'Môn Mam Cymru' lingers, despite changing fortunes in the twentieth century. For the phrase, which means 'Anglesey the mother of Wales', refers back to the days when Ynys Môn (Anglesey) supplied the North Wales mainland with food in times of hardship or siege. True to tradition, the island's way of life has been that of the farmer-producer rather than the seafarer. In prehistoric times, tribes began to cultivate the island and remains of their settlements can be found at Bryn Celli Ddu near Llanddaniel Fab in the south and at Din Llugwy between Benllech and Amlwch. It was, however, the later Celtic culture which has been influential, perhaps more so than the Roman invasion of AD 60 onwards. It is said that the early Druids of the island brought trepidation to the invading Roman soldiers.

The earthworks of Celtic settlements at Cwr y Twr at Holyhead mountain or Din Sylwy north-east of Llandonna village as well as numerous standing stones, circles and wells which all survive throughout the island indicate the dominance of the ancient cultures.

Gently lies the land of Ynys Môn. There is no high ground here except for the soaring cliffs of the west coast where ancient pre-Cambrian strata, folded well over 600 million years ago, hold back the relentless tide of the sea. The island landscape is more reflective of the limestone beds around Traeth-coch (Red Wharf Bay) or the softer carboniferous layers reaching down to the south-eastern coastline. The last ice age, depositing boulder clay and gravels, has moulded an undulating landscape broken only by outcrop and ridge as land approaches sea. Rivers, such as the Briant and the Cefni, flow mainly in a south-easterly direction. Very little wetland survives, the most extensive area being the Malltraeth marsh, south of Llangefni.

Despite intensive farming wildlife habitats survive thanks to the work of organisations such as the North Wales Wildlife Trust and the Royal Society for the Protection of Birds (RSPB). The coastline is magnificent for birds; oyster catchers, redshanks and plovers can be readily observed, as can migratory birds such as guillemots, razor-bills, puffins and cormorants who come to breed. The RSPB centre at South Stack on Ynys Gybi (best approached along the coastal path) is an exceptional site especially during the main breeding time of late May to early July, but there are other coastal sites of interest such as Ynys Llanddwyn, brimming with wild flowers. Children love the many beaches of Ynys Môn to look for shells and crabs amongst the rock pools or to roam in the surrounding dunes colonised by grasses and scrub. Try Aberffraw, Llanddwyn or Traeth-coch for a very special seaside outing.

Only small remnants of deciduous woodland survive, as well as some parkland from Victorian estates along the Menai Straits, but for the most part conifer plantations such as the large pine forest of Newborough have been planted in recent years.

Ynys Môn is also a stronghold of Welsh culture as embodied in the Welsh language. Throughout the century the island has enjoyed the work of talented Welsh poets and musicians and to a lesser extent painters. Kyffin Williams, a well known twentieth century Welsh painter, resides here. The concern of the 1990s is how to retain this distinctive culture given the large influx of retired people from the north-west of England. Several North Wales organisations such as Cymdeithas yr Iaith Gymraeg (The Welsh Language Society) and Cyngor y Dysgwyr (The Learners' Council) continue to fight for their cultural identity, as have their ancestors over the centuries, and Welsh language courses are well subscribed on the island.

The population is sparse, however, and most people live in the small towns and villages. Caergybi (Holyhead), as a major port to Eire, is the largest settlement, with a population of between 14,000 and 15,000. Its fortunes have always been tied to sea trade. Caergybi is a busy place at times, not at all pretentious like the triumphal arch built to signify the end of the A5 road from London, but functional. The pedestrianised shopping area is pleasant but the narrow streets feeding down to the harbour are more interesting.

Other interesting towns include Amlwch, once a small fishing port but changed by the copper mining at nearby Parys Mountain. The little inlet, Porth Amlwch, to the northeast of the town centre is of interest. Beaumaris, with its massive Edwardian castle of World Heritage Site status with its surrounding charming streets is as popular now as it was with the Victorians who thought it very fashionable. Nearby is Menai Bridge town which has since the bridging of the Menai Straits been a crossroads for the traveller. Benllech and Rhosneigr are seaside resorts while Bodedern, Llannerch-y-Medd and Llangefni are small towns of character, the latter being the busiest market and administrative centre. They are reasonably well linked by Bws Gwynedd or train.

The villages of Ynys Môn are a storehouse of culture, homes to bards and others, surrounded by legends and yarns, offering a quiet retreat from busy roads. Getting to them by bus requires a little more time and planning but in most instances is possible. Cycling the back lanes will bring you to places like Brynsiencyn, which was an important centre in prehistoric times, to the harbour village of Cemaes, or to Llanddona in search of the legendary witches. Wherever you go, the quieter parts of the island bring a rich reward.

**Tourist information:** Caergybi Tourist Information Centre, Salt Island, Caergybi (0407) 762622; Llanfairpwll Tourist Information Centre, Llanfairpwll Railway Station (0248) 713177.

**Transport:** British Rail run an InterCity service through to Caergybi and a stopping service to local stations in the south of the island, including the re-opened Llanfairpwllgwyngyllgogerychyrndrobwll-llantysiliogogogoch station, a name first used in the last century as a publicity stunt, with long lasting effects. The bus network is run mainly by Crosville Wales and the local company Lewis at Llanerch-y-medd. Gwynedd County Council produce a timetable leaflet for Ynys Môn and an excellent route map for the entire county, which is available from Tourist Information Centres.

There are two cycle hire centres, one at Bryn Coed, Llanfaelog near Rhosneigr (0407) 810227, the other at Brynteg (0248) 853479 which is also an activity centre.

Island Ranger Expeditions at Traeth-coch (0248) 70789 offer Island Ranger Mystical Isle Holidays by Land Rover with a local guide. Ynys Môn Walking Holidays, Amlwch (0407) 831493 arrange guided and self-guided walking packages.

**Access to the countryside:** In recent years work has continued to improve footpaths on the island and the coastal path is ideal for walking from local villages to nature reserves and ancient monuments. On the outskirts of Caergybi is Penrhos Coastal Park owned by the Aluminium Smelting Company. There are good local walks around the salt marshes and pools of Malltraeth (Bws Gwynedd 42) or along the canalised River Cefni. To the south is the nature reserve of Ynys Llanddwyn and Newborough Warren (Bws Gwynedd 42, 53), both offering interesting rambles. There are pleasant walks from Benllech (Bws Gwynedd 61, 62, 63) to Llanbedr-Goch where there are nature reserves managed by the North Wales Wildlife Trust at Cors Goch and Craig Wen.

Near Llangefni is Cefni reservoir which is popular with local birdwatchers and on the north-west coast a walk from Cemaes (Bws Gwynedd 61, 62A) leads to Cemlyn Lagoon, a natural bar and pool which attracts a variety of waterfowl. At Llys Llywelyn near Aberffraw (Bws Gwynedd 42) is the Anglesey Coastal Heritage Centre, offering guided walks. There are boat trips on the Starida from Beaumaris to Puffin Island, but they do not land as this uninhabited island is a nature reserve.

There is also Hen Blas Country Park (0407) 840152 near Bodorgan (Bws Gwynedd 42), very much geared to children. Open farms include Bryntirion farm (0248) 430232 at Dwyran (Bws Gwynedd 42) and Farm Life at Bodowyr near Bodedern (0407) 741171 (Bws Gwynedd 46). Other countryside-based attractions are Anglesey Sea Zoo, displaying local underwater species, at Brynsiencyn (0248) 430411 (Bws Gwynedd 42), and Llynnon working windmill at Llandeusant (0407) 730797 (Bws Gwynedd 60).

**Museums:** The Holyhead Maritime Museum tells a yarn or two about the town's seafaring tradition. There is a small and delightful Museum of Childhood in Castle Street, Beaumaris which features toys and games of by-gone times. Other historic attractions with displays include Beaumaris Gaol which offers an insight into Victorian punitive measures, and Beaumaris Courthouse. In the same town is Third Eye in Church Street, a museum of craft and trade tools once used by shipwrights and coopers. The restaurant here places emphasis on vegetarian dishes. The stately home of Plas Newydd (Bws Gwynedd 42), bordering the Menai Straits, and Hen Blas at Llangristiolus, a seventeenth-century manor house, are also open to the public, as is Penmon Priory and Dovecote (Bws Gwynedd 56). The Stone Science Centre, Bryn Eglwys, Llanddyfnan (0248) 70310 exhibits a range of fossils, minerals and archaeological material.

**Craft workshops:** In Ynys Môn tradition there are a number of craft workshops throughout the island. The Bodeilio Craft Centre at Talwrn (0248) 722535 near Llangefni (Bws Gwynedd 50) specialises in small-scale designer knitwear, as does Rhoscolyn Knitwear on Holy Island (0407) 860681, and uses Welsh wool. The latter is along the coast from Trearddur, a lovely walk. There is an Anglesey Craftworkers Guild which produce goods for sale throughout the island, details from Mrs C. Edwards, Tyn-y-Cae, Hedsor Idan, Brynsiencyn. There are several art galleries, of which one of the most interesting is Oriel Fach, Castle Street, Beaumaris, where local artists display work.

**Wholefoods:** While many places now serve a vegetarian dish or two, Caffi'r Bont at Menai Bridge and The Whole Thing at Llangefni both specialise in wholefoods.

**Health:** Peacock Herbs near Llanerch-y-medd (0248) 470231 specialises in culinary, medicinal and aromatic herb plants. There is a natural medicine clinic, Natural Ways, at Caergeiliog (0407) 741297.

**Co-operatives:** Cwmni Pentref Llanfairpwll Village Cooperative provides an umbrella organisation for economic development.

**Energy:** The Wylfa nuclear power station near Cemaes, has been the subject of much protest.

**Community initiatives:** Anglesey Coastal Heritage encourages community involvement in conservation of the island's coastline. Theatr Fach at Llangefni encourages local productions with concerts in both Welsh and English.

# Coastal resorts
# of North Wales

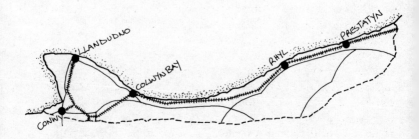

This slip of land sandwiched between the daunting foothills of Yr Eryri and the Irish Sea, sliced by rail and road and festooned with caravans, would appear at first sight to hold little for the Green traveller. Not wholly correct, as for those who enjoy the sea air and the feel of a seaside resort there is much to offer. Furthermore, a few miles beyond these natural and man-made barriers is a gently undulating Clwyd with villages and hamlets tucked away from the seaside bustle, offering a soothing respite from the more crowded locations. In fact, the limestone ridges running south into the hills from the more intensively cultivated lowlands give way to mixed farming and pleasant open country with fine views out to sea.

Given that the coastline is so crowded, however, there is little room left for wildlife, although the dunes running from Prestatyn to the Dee estuary and the headlands of Colwyn and Llandudno support a varied birdlife, as does the limited remaining marsh area of the Afon Clwyd. Little woodland remains and thus the nature trail at Bryn Euryn, Colwyn Bay, the southern flanks of Abergele and the woodland around Prestatyn make a welcome break.

The resorts of Prestatyn, Rhyl, Abergele and Colwyn Bay have geared themselves to a mass market, people seeking a mix of modern entertainment in a traditional seaside town. The fortunes of these places have been erratic, and it shows, but if it is a seaside base you seek, they do offer miles of sand, sea and fresh air although not many of the beaches are given any beach awards.

Of the resorts Llandudno is by far the most elegant. Not only has it endeavoured to retain its Victorian charm, it has striven to maintain high standards of cleanliness despite the deluge of visitors during the summer months. The North Shore beach, for example, is the only one in the area to be given a mention in *The Good Beach Guide*. The restoration of the pier is excellent, although some of the retailing outlets do not quite match the overall image intended. Let us hope the tram system to the Great Orme flourishes, as it is a unique feature in the area and allows easy access for everyone to the Great Orme Country Park, a magnificent headland projecting into the Irish Sea. Other parts of Llandudno's tramways (more properly known as the electric railway) are no longer in existence, more is the pity.

Conwy looks magnificent from across the waters despite the paraphernalia of twentieth-century communications. Following a major consultancy report in recent years Conwy is seeking to establish itself as a visitor destination of international repute. The castle and town walls are, after all, rather special, as are the narrow streets of medieval dimension. It would also be good to see the harbour more as a working port, thus retaining some balance, but this seems unlikely. Conwy, without traffic congestion, is a place of distinction – as is Llandudno, despite its penchant for extolling its relationship with the famous author Lewis Carroll. Together the two towns form a good base for a holiday break and allow ready access to Snowdonia.

**Tourist information:** Colwyn Bay Tourist Information Centre, Station Road (0492) 530478; Conwy Tourist Information Centre,

Conwy Castle (0492) 592248; Llandudno Tourist Information Centre, Chapel Street (0492) 76413; Prestatyn Tourist Information Centre (07456) 4365; Rhyl Tourist Information Centre (0745) 355068.

**Transport:** British Rail serves most of the resorts with a daily service; Crosville Wales is the major bus operator in this area with regular services to most places. With their wide range of tickets from the Bws Gwynedd Rover to Crosville's own Weekly Rover they allow the traveller to get out into the countryside and a surprising number of services in the summer allow for a good day out to quite remote parts. For information contact Crosville Wales on (0492) 596969. For services in the eastern part of this area you might also have to consult Bws Clwyd on (0352) 2121 ext. 4035.

West End Cycles (0492) 518578 at Old Colwyn offers cycle hire and Rhyl can be seen by rickshaw during the season!

**Access to the countryside:** Besides walks along the seafront at the resorts there are a number of local walks into the quieter countryside along the coastal fringe. Prestatyn is the start of Offa's Dyke Path and there is a local walk in the 'Walks in Clwyd' series by Gordon Emery featuring Gop Hill and Trelwanyd. The hills around Meliden and Dyserth provide a number of short walks, dotted as they are with prehistoric remnants. Pick up the walks sheet from Prestatyn Tourist Information Centre. The waterfalls at Dyserth are popular. Between Abergele and Colwyn Bay the back lanes and footpaths provide an escape into the countryside, once you are across the A55 road. There are two local nature trails, one at Pwllycrochan, Upper Colwyn Bay and the other at Bryn Euryn, Rhos-on-Sea, for which leaflets are available at local Tourist Information Offices.

The Great Orme Country Park, a superb grassy summit in Llandudno, offers a sense of space and light. There are guided walks from the visitor centre during the summer. The best way is to travel up by the tramway from Victoria station, perhaps walking down to the West Shore and Deganwy. One nearby attraction is Bodnant Gardens (Bws Gwynedd 25, 65) with its enticing range of trees from throughout the world. Conwy is the starting point for local walks up to the summit of Mynydd-y-Dref (Conwy Mountain).

**Museums:** Conwy Castle must be one of the finest Edwardian castles in Wales, and what a setting. Rapallo House in Llandudno is both museum and gallery with a range of exhibitions. Lewis Carroll, the author of *Alice in Wonderland*, is associated with Llandudno and this has given rise to an Alice in Wonderland Visitor Centre. Rhyl Museum and Arts Centre contains local history exhibitions. Bodelwyddan Castle contains museum displays and part of the National Portrait Gallery. During the summer a free bus serves the castle from Rhyl railway station (0745) 584060. Another short outing from Rhyl takes the visitor to St. Asaph Cathedral and Museum, the smallest cathedral in Britain.

**Craft workshops:** There are a number of commercial gift shop cum craft centres in the resorts.

**Wholefoods:** The Granary at Conwy sells wholefoods and Food For Good in Rhyl Library and Museum is a co-operative based cafe offering a wholefood menu. The International Indian Restaurant at Llandudno Junction serves vegetarian dishes, as do several of the hotels such as The Grafton and St. Tudno in Llandudno. The Whole in the Wall, The Promenade, Rhos-on-Sea offers wholefoods. In Abergele there is a wholefood outlet at Nature's Way, Market Street.

**Community initiatives:** Canopy, an umbrella group concerned with peace and conservation can be contacted at Nant yr Efail, Glan Conwy, near Colwyn Bay.

# Llŷn Peninsula

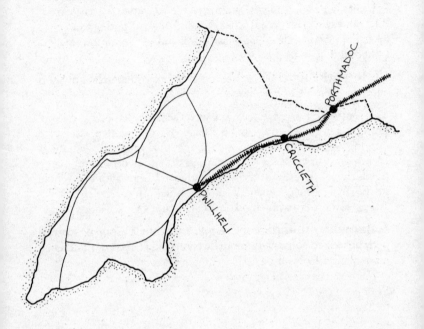

The Llŷn Peninsula is beautiful. The tapering finger of landscape, visited through the centuries by pilgrims in their search for Ynys Enlli (Bardsey Island), has until recent decades been largely untouched. Even the Victorians, with their belief that civilisation could only be possible if a railway was built, failed to make an impression beyond Pwllheli. This rich and varied landscape has done well to resist being overwhelmed by recent tourism. Perhaps its relative isolation, regardless of the motor car, will be its saviour.

The making of the peninsula is certainly a reflection of central Yr Eryri (Snowdonia) in a geological sense, hard igneous rocks surrounded by softer sedimentary deposits which weather far more easily. Even so, it is a lowland landscape in that the igneous outcrops, molten masses which cooled and contorted millions of years ago, are few in relation to the miles of softer smoothed rocks, partially clothed in boulder clays of the glacial and post-glacial eras. There is something of an erratic backbone of hills, but where harder rocks meet the sea there are prominent headlands which look impressive on a summer's evening as the sun sets.

It is this varied landscape that has led to an equally varied wildlife. Very little indigenous mixed woodland remains however, and farming is dominated by sheep and cattle grazing on the lower pastures. The cliffs are of major interest to the conservationist and are now the focus of a heritage project. In many areas they are little disturbed and birds come to nest without hindrance.

Celtic culture flourished in these parts, and the hills are littered with the remains of earlier prehistoric communities in the shape of burial chambers, hut circles, forts and possibly an axe factory at Mynydd Rhiw. There appears to have been a real concentration of communities in the southern half of the Llŷn Peninsula perhaps through the combination of high hills for security and close proximity to the coast. Very few of the sites were later colonised by medieval lords, as happened more frequently elsewhere, so the peninsula does not possess the massive castles of Edward I. There are many climbs up to the ancient sites, with magnificent views seaward.

For centuries, the major economic activities of the area have been fishing and farming. The former has virtually disappeared and tourism has taken its place in towns like Pwllheli and Abersoch. They are, nevertheless, full of character. Most non-car travellers arrive at Pwllheli railway station, which was at one time such a busy terminus. Witness the long platforms which make the Sprinters look embarrassingly small on arrival. Walking into the town there is the bustle expected from a market and administrative centre. From here the Green traveller journeys, like the earlier pilgrims, through coastal resorts such as Llanbedrog and Abersoch or Morfa Nefyn, which while being very popular still retain a relaxed air that is lost in larger resorts.

The villages are the bastion of the Welsh culture here, places like Llithfaen with walks up to the ancient hill fort of Tre'r-Ceir, Rhiw beneath Mynydd Rhiw, Llangwnnadl and its chapel nestled in a wooded vale and Uwchymynydd, ever looking out to the sea. Aberdaron is the last port of call before Ynys Enlli, and Y Gegin

Fawr, now a cafe and shop, was once the place where pilgrims waited for the right tide to cross to the mystical isle.

Also part of the Llŷn Peninsula are the towns and villages surrounding Porthmadog, a town brought to fame through the export of slate by sea. The Ffestiniog Railway brought the slate down from Blaenau Ffestiniog and the building of the Cob embankment to Porthmadog harbour changed the landscape considerably. Nearby Tremadog was also the creation of the Madocks family who invested so much in the area, so that oceangoing schooners could ship out slate to the four corners of the world.

A different sort of architectural achievement can be seen at Portmeirion across the Cob. Created by the architect Sir William Clough-Ellis, this dream village in windswept woodland is an example of how architecture is meant to blend with and even enhance a surrounding area of natural beauty. Through the decades, Portmeirion has become home to a range of reconstructed buildings transported from elsewhere.

Criccieth is a welcoming small resort between Porthmadog and Pwllheli with the only major castle of note in the area. It is also a good base for visiting the countless villages, open spaces and farms in the gentler flowing landscape between the coast and the foothills of Yr Eryri (Snowdonia). Not that the town itself is without interest. Once off the main road it is a reserved and gentle place with many old farms and mills, some still raising stock, others diversifying as the pressure to shift from dairying continues. It is a paradise for those who like to get off the beaten track.

**Tourist information:** Abersoch Tourist Information Centre (0758) 812929; Porthmadog Tourist Information Centre, High Street (0766) 512981; Pwllheli Tourist Information Centre, Y Maes (0758) 613000.

**Transport:** Porthmadog, Criccieth and Pwllheli are served by British Rail's Cambrian Coast line, a scenic route par excellence, running up the coast from Dovey Junction near Machynlleth to Pwllheli. The Ffestiniog narrow gauge steam railway provides a marvellous journey to Porthmadog from Blaenau Ffestiniog for those wishing to travel to the Llŷn Peninsula by way of the North Wales coast.

There are also connecting buses from Llandudno to Porthmadog and Portmeirion (part of Snowdon Sherpa) which traverse a spectacular route via Beddgelert. The main bus routes from the northwest are Bws Gwynedd route 1 from Caernarfon to Porthmadog and route 12 from Caernarfon to Pwllheli.

Local towns and villages in the Llŷn Peninsula are also served by Bws Gwynedd and Gwynedd County Council produces a local bus timetable leaflet covering the Dwyfor area which includes these services. Services for the most part run hourly during the day, but there are few buses in the evenings and on Sundays. Crosville Wales is the main operator. There are a number of smaller companies such as Clynnog & Trefor and Express.

Cycling in the area is good fun if you can avoid the main road summer traffic. Go for the back lanes. The Lôn Eifion cycle route along the Pwllheli to Caernarfon railway is ideal for starters. Leafy Lanes Cycle Hire at Ysgubor Fawr, Chwilog (0766) 810518 provide cycle hire and cycle holiday packages. They also arrange practical skills courses for beginners in plumbing, carpentry, etc. since according to the owners 'the case is often that mum learns plumbing whilst dad takes the children cycling'!

Zena Holidays International (0766) 85638 of Penrhyndeudraeth offer study cum activity holidays such as walking and canoeing as well as ecological and Green studies.

**Access to the countryside:** The Llŷn Peninsula is beautiful and what better way to enjoy it than leaving the bicycle behind and taking off on foot. The footpath network along the coast is being improved so walking between villages, perhaps using the local bus or train on the outward or return leg of the journey, is a good way of discovering the peninsula. The Llŷn Heritage Coast Project, established in 1985, has attempted through footpath improvements and information to aim for a balance between conservation and the increasing pressure of the visitor. One longer walk linking Minfford and Criccieth by way of the Cob, Porthmadog Harbour, Borth-y-Gest and Black Rock sands is described in *Great Walks from Welsh Railways* by Lumsdon and Speakman (Sigma Press) and makes for a splendid day's walking.

Bodvel Hall Farm Park (0758) 613386, on Bws Gwynedd route 8, includes an open farm area and nature walks as well as more commercial ventures. Gwynfryn farm (0758) 612536, which has not used artificial fertilisers or spray on the land for eighteen years, arranges farm visits and has holiday cottages to rent. Portmeirion illustrates just how a site can be developed for commercial purposes without destroying the very features which attract the visitor, but as it is strictly commercial there is an entrance charge. It is a mile from Minfford which is served by rail and Bws Gwynedd routes 1 and 2, but from April to October Bws Gwynedd 97 runs up to the entrance to Portmeirion village (0766) 770228. There are miles of walking throughout the wooded estate to secluded beaches.

**Museums:** The Lloyd George Museum (0766) 522071 at Llanystumdwy near Criccieth (Bws Gwynedd 2) is an unusual attraction. There is also a self-guided village trail around the village. Another interesting place to visit is the Maritime Museum (0766) 513736 at Oakley Wharf, Porthmadog, reflecting how the port was built to export slate throughout the world. Other museums in the area are the Llŷn Historical and Maritime Museum (0758) 720308 at Nefyn and the Motor Museum (0766) 512098 at Porthmadog. The quarrying and transport of slate is part of the story on both the Ffestiniog Railway (0766) 512340 and the Welsh Highland Railway situated by Porthmadog British Rail station.

**Bookshops:** Browsers Bookshop in Porthmadog has a large selection of books including a range on the environment. Siop Eifonydd in Porthmadog specialises in Welsh books, as does Llen Llŷn in Y Maes, Pwllheli. The Bookseller in Pwllheli and Zebra Books in Criccieth have a range of conservation and local books.

**Craft workshops:** Tyn Llan Crafts have converted old farm buildings and quiet though it seems now, the old road passing the farm was busy at one time with pilgrims journeying to Ynys Enlli (Bardsey Island) and drovers taking cattle to Porthmadog. It is a short walk from Penmorfa village which is on Bws Gwynedd routes 1 and 2. J.M. Crafts at Bryn Llewelyn, Botwnnog (075 883) 245, nearest route Bws Gwynedd 17, makes jewellery and traditional slate work. Cwm Pottery near Trefor (028 686) 545 produces a wide range of fired stoneware (Bws Gwynedd 12). Brynkir Woollen Mill at Golan (Bws Gwynedd 1) was originally built to grind corn but was converted in the last century to woollen manufacture and you can see the products being made for sale in the shop. Locally-born painter Rob Piercy has an interesting gallery in Snowdon Street, Porthmadog (0766) 513833, and the Oriel Gallery at Plas Glyn-y-Weddw (0758) 740763 near Llanbedrog has been beautifully presented by Welsh artist Gwyneth ap Thomos and her husband Davydd. Oriel Penlan in Penlan, Pwllheli, exhibits mainly local artists and crafts.

**Wholefoods:** Siop Newydd and Iechyd Da are both on the High Street in Criccieth. Iechyd Da at Mitre Terrace, Pwllheli and The Wholefood Shop in the High Street, Pwllheli sell wholesome fare, the latter being proud of its muesli. The Tasty Food Shop on Harbour Road, Abersoch also offers wholefoods and there is a well-known restaurant, The Islander, at Lôn Sarn Bach which also offers bed and breakfast. Y Llong or The Ship Inn in Lombard Street at Porthmadog offers vegetarian, Thai and Malaysian dishes and Blossoms at Borth-y-Gest makes vegetarians welcome.

**Co-operatives:** Cwmni Tŷ Newydd at Pwllheli is a community co-operative umbrella for a co-operative pub.

**Community initiatives:** Llŷn Heritage Coast Project encourages conservation along the coastline of the peninsula which is designated an Area of Outstanding Natural Beauty. The Project Officer is based with the borough authority, Cyngor Dosbarth Dwyfor (0758) 613131.

'Naturally Gwynedd' is a recent scheme launched by Gwynedd County Council to create more awareness of Green issues in the county.

There is an active Friends of the Earth group which can be contacted on (075 883) 423.

The Greenpeace group for Gwynedd, Clwyd and Powys can be contacted on (0754) 687765.

Nant Gwrteyrn National Language Centre, Llithfaen (0758) 85334 provides a centre for learning Welsh language and culture, offering short residential courses and other facilities. There is also the Tŷ Newydd Language Centre at Llanystumdwy (0766) 522811. The Snowdonia Steiner School at Tan Yr Allt, Tremadog is an educational establishment, the gardening group of which is cultivating a walled garden using bio-dynamic methods. Workshop programmes are available (0766) 512068.

# *Yr Eryri – Snowdonia*

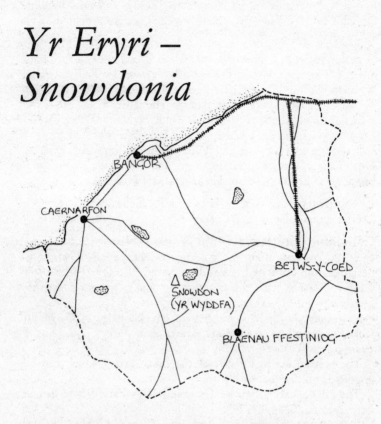

Yr Eryri (Snowdonia) is a remarkable place. Barely populated even to this day, except for the old slate towns of the last century, these ancient mountains are still remote. Ironically, they attracted the travel writers of two centuries ago simply because they were seen as such a challenge, only to be penetrated via rugged packhorse trails and the peaks themselves on foot. Thanks to one particular writer, Thomas Pennant, who walked by night to the summit of Yr Wyddfa (Snowdon) to arrive at dawn, an entourage of would-be discoverers followed in his footsteps, literary characters seeking adventure and fame. But it was not their doing that Yr Eryri (Snowdonia) has subsequently been opened up; it was mainly because of the demands of the quarrying giants of the day who were seeking to extract and despatch as much slate and rock and as many minerals as possible to the outside world.

The geology of the area is not easy to follow. Imagine 600-700 million years ago some of the oldest rocks in the world being formed, now known as pre-Cambrian, very compressed and hard. Not only these, but also much younger but nevertheless weather-resistant rocks, twisted and contorted into peaks and dips during the Ordivician period, and later thrust up from massive oceans to be subjected to millions of years of erosion. This was compounded by the work of glaciers during more recent ice ages, gouging out cwms or corrie lakes and moulding u shaped valleys such as Nant Ffrancon and Llanberis, leaving residual lakes such as Padarn and Gwynant.

The result is a range of magnificent mountains, truncated by wide valleys and narrow passes, with shoulder foothills giving way to a narrow coastal strip of fertile soils and maritime settlements. The wildlife is as varied as the landscape itself. Parc Cenedlaethol Eryri (Snowdonia National Park) has a remit to conserve this wildlife in conjunction with local farmers and us. The land is grazed mainly by sheep and to a much lesser degree cattle. The other major land use is forestry and much of the wood planted is coniferous rather than the native oaklands of centuries ago. This concerns conservationists, as wildlife is far less rich in the vast tracts of these plantations. Furthermore, what survives of the old oaklands is under threat given the increased grazing by sheep. This hinders the regeneration process as sheep nibble away the seedlings. Furthermore there is the rhododendron menace, a plant which starves all others in its rampant colonisation of habitats.

There is, of course, a diversity of habitats within close proximity, in the same way that the underlying rock structures are complex. The poor acid soils and marshland of the high mountains lead to alpine vegetation so that reindeer moss and fescue grass are common, lichens grow in nooks and crannies, and alpine cinquefoil, bistort and saw wort can be readily found. Predatory birds – the kestrel, buzzard and carrion crow – hover over small mammals and young sheep. This contrasts with the wetter, more sheltered valleys such as the Lledr where bluebells, wood sorrel and a host of other plants survive in the oak remnants.

In terms of settlements most are on the old coaching routes of the last two centuries. Before then, in the time of the Welsh princes, most of the area was barely settled and not much touched by ruling groups. It is along one of the early lines of communication that the Green traveller is likely to go. The coastal settlements of Conwy, Penmaenmawr, Bangor and Caernarfon were not only ports but also defensive positions, as witnessed by their castles. Bangor and Caernarfon have real character, not destroyed by the demands of this century. They also form the gateway to the smaller more tourist-orientated communities on the high ground, Beddgelert and Llanberis. The former is less spoilt, regardless of those who come to see the grave of Llywelyn's faithful hound, supposedly slain by mistake after defending the infant heir from a wolf, a lovely yarn which everyone wants to believe. Llanberis, where the train leaves for the summit has in recent years developed a number of attractions and has become far more popular. Future proposals for tourism development have become a real issue.

The other way into Yr Eryri is by way of the Conwy Valley to Llanwrst, still very much a Welsh market town of character, and then to Betws-y-Coed. Beautiful it is, lying not much above sea level and yet surrounded by high mountains and the fresh pine forests of the Gwydyr. The trouble is that too many of us arrive at the same time and take the paths to the very scenic Swallow Falls, then mope through the collection of gift shops on the main thoroughfare afterwards. Go for the quieter walks in the Lledr Valley or the Upper Conwy near Penmachno and it is a world apart.

Finally, the slate towns add a decidedly unusual feel to the area. Arriving at Blaenau Ffestiniog by train for the first time is quite a shock, with mountains of slate surrounding the town. The story of the mines and their heritage is well told, often by ex-miners who know what life was really like down there. The temptation is to travel from these high mountains to the coast on the Ffestiniog steam railway, and indeed what better way to leave Yr Eryri.

**Tourist information:** Bangor Tourist Information Office, Theatr Gwynedd (0248) 352786; Betws-y-Coed Tourist Information Office, Royal Oak Stables (0690) 710426; Caernarfon, Oriel Pendeitsh (0286) 672232; Llanberis, Oriel Eryri (0286) 870765.

**Transport:** British Rail runs a service along the North Wales coast to Llanfairfechan, Penmaenmawr and Bangor. The main interchange point for Yr Eryri (Snowdonia) is Llandudno Junction, where a beautiful branch line runs up the serene Conwy valley to Betws-y-Coed and then climbs more dramatically to the terminus at

Blaenau Ffestiniog. From here the Ffestiniog railway operates to Porthmadog. The other major interchange is at Bangor, where there are buses for Bethesda, Caernarfon, Dinorwic and Llanberis. Caernarfon, however, is the main hub of the bus network into Yr Eryri. The Snowdon Sherpa network is one of the best ways to see Yr Eryri and it generally operates from early April through to late October.

The Gwynedd Bus Rover and Crosville Wales Day Rover ticket is excellent value for money and there is a range of Crosville Wales tickets valid for longer periods. The co-ordination of bus services under the general banner of Bws Gwynedd is so good that it makes it feasible to visit many places, so wherever possible the routes have been listed.

Cycling in these rugged parts is not as daunting as you might first think. With the new designs of bicycles with umpteen gears, hills become less of a struggle. There are cycle hire centres at Bangor, Steve's Cycles, High Street (0248) 361400; at Llanberis, The Llanberis Bike Centre, High Street (0286) 871534; and at Betws-y-Coed, Beics Betws, Tan Lan Cafe (0690) 710766. The Lôn Eifion cycle route, designed and managed by Gwynedd County Council, runs from Caernarfon to Bryncir and is well worth the ride. There are cycle hire centres nearby: 14th Peak, Palace Street, Caernarfon (0286) 5124 hire cycles as do Gwern, Saron, Llanwanda (0286) 831337, both places being close to the cycle route. Another exciting project is Lôn Bach, a cycle route between Bangor and Bethesda – see Community initiatives.

**Access to the countryside:** The Parc Cenedlaethol Eryri (Snowdonia National Park) offers so many opportunities for walking, with paths being clear and well-marked in the more popular areas. Footpaths between railway stations, such as Dolwyddelan to Pont-y-Pant and Betws-y-Coed to Llanwrst, offer pleasant easy rambles. Gwynedd County Council produces a series of local walks leaflets including Caerhun in the Conwy Valley and the Panoramic Walk at Penmaenmawr. The National Park usually publishes a leaflet outlining a programme of guided walks throughout the season. There are dozens of booklets and leaflets illustrating local walks such as Barry Horton's *Ten Walks from Blaenau Ffestiniog*, and these are available at shops and Tourist Information Centres. There are also several imaginative walking holiday packages on offer from firms such as Spectrum Walks (0766) 830511, Dolawel Guest

55

House, Blaenau Ffestiniog. Another way to explore is by river with Conwy Canoe Tours (0492) 596457.

On the northern edge of the Park is a grand walk over the Sychnant Pass to Conwy which is lengthy, but many short walks are possible from Penmaenmawr and Llanfairfechan. A few miles beyond is the village of Aber (served by the Crosville Cymru Coastliner or Bws Gwynedd 5) and a short walk into the foothills leads to a local nature trail and then on to Aber Falls. South of Caernarfon is Parc Glynllifon (Bws Gwynedd 1, 2, 80 and 86) which offers walks in historic gardens to a Victorian hermitage and other fascinating spots. Nearby is Merlin's Park Wildlife Conservation Reserve (Bws Gwynedd 12). At Betws Garmon are Hafodty Gardens (Bws Gwynedd 11) which are a joy to walk in, as are the woods surrounding Beddgelert. There is also the Cae Du farm park (076 686) 345 nearby.

Most, however, seek out a journey through Llanberis Pass to the town of Llanberis and look for ways up Yr Wyddfa (Snowdon) itself, which should be treated with utter respect despite the thousands who climb it from different angles. For those not too keen on scrambles, a ramble from The Snowdon Ranger youth hostel to the south (Bws Gwynedd 11) or the Beddgelert path (same bus) from Pitts Head might be the best bet as others such as the Pen-y-Grwd and Miners Track approaching from the north and west are harder. The starting points are all served by the Snowdon Sherpa bus network. If you do not have the appropriate outdoor clothing or the stamina, use the Snowdon mountain railway from Llanberis, an exhilarating journey in its own right on Britain's only rack and pinion mountain railway.

Padarn Country Park on the shores of Llyn Padarn offers local walks or a ride on the Llanberis Lake railway. There are numerous nature trails in the area, as at Bethania in Nant Gwynant and in the Nant Ffrancon pass.

**Museums:** The Old Canonry in Bangor illustrates mainly crafts and furniture-making in earlier centuries. Bangor Cathedral is thought to be the oldest cathedral in continuous use in Wales if not Britain. A mile from the city is Penrhyn Castle which contains a doll museum and an industrial railway museum. The restored Victorian pier adds to the character of the town.

Caernarfon is steeped in history with the museum at the Roman fort Segontium and the Edwardian castle guarding the straits. Many of the town walls remain, as does the old harbour. Nearby will be found the Seiont II Maritime Museum. Not far south is the Museum of Welsh Country Life at Tai'n Lon, Clynnog Fawr (0286) 86311. There is no bus service but it is a lovely walk from Aberdesach village on Bws Gwynedd 12, which is part of a restored corn mill. At Beddgelert is the Sygun Copper mine (0766) 86595 which the Snowdon Sherpa passes.

There is a Welsh Slate Museum at Llanberis near to the Dinorwic hydro-electric power station. New to the area is The Museum of the North, based on the theme of power in past ages and with modern technology courtesy of the National Grid. The place to see the results of slate production is Blaenau Ffestiniog, which has two fascinating former slate mines, Gloddfa Ganol and Llechwedd, open to the public and telling a very realistic tale about mining. The Conwy Valley Railway Museum at Betws-y-Coed railway station is of interest to model railway enthusiasts.

**Bookshops:** There are two interesting bookshops in Caernarfon; The Palace Bookshop in Pool Street, and Gray Thomas in Pendeitsh.

**Craft workshops:** Traditional slate-working can be seen at Inigo Jones (0286) 830242 which is probably the last surviving example of a fully operational slate works in North Wales, at Groeslon south of Caernarfon on Bws Gwynedd routes 1, 2, 80 and 86. In the Conwy valley, Trefiw Woollen Mill near Llanwrst (0492) 640462 on Bws Gwynedd 64 and Penmachno Mill (06902) 545, hidden among wooded valleys and plunging streams, are well worth visiting. Near Penmachno village is Tŷ Mawr, the birthplace of Bishop Morgan who first translated the Bible into Welsh.

**Wholefoods:** 'Herbs' in Mount Street, Bangor offers vegetarian take-away food and a dining room. In Caernarfon try Harvest at The Wellfield Centre, Caernarfon Cottage Kitchen in Eastgate Street and Just Natural, Pool Hill. The Bubbling Kettle at Betws-y-Coed offers good food amid a sea of fast food. Siop Gwerdd, High Street, Blaenau Ffestiniog has a range of wholefoods.

**Health:** The spa at Trefiw (0492) 640057 is said to produce the richest medicinal chalybeate spa water in the world.

**Co-operatives:** There are a number of interesting co-operatives in the area including Cadwaith Cyf at Trawsfynydd (within proximity of the omnipresent nuclear power station) which aims to create employment through conservation. At Bethesda Cytgord Cyf, a public information service specialises in promoting Welsh rock music. Hywl y Fflag (0248) 351140 is a Welsh language theatre company.

## Community initiatives:
Naturally Gwynedd, jointly sponsored by Gwynedd County Council and the Wales Tourist Board, aims to make residents and visitors more aware of what Gwynedd has to offer in terms of Green tourism.

Gwynedd Cycleroutes, Tŷ Gwydr, Fford Clynnog, Penygroes, Caernarfon (0286) 881009 aims to build a series of cycle routes, including Lôn Bach, throughout the county and is involved with a cross country route to Cardiff. What a beautiful thought!

The North Wales Wildlife Trust has a shop in High Street, Bangor and there is a Community Information Centre called Greenhouse in Trevelyan Terrace.

Cynlas, an alternative community living at Rhos Isaf collectively maintains an organic smallholding as well as having members working on a self-employed basis at other things.

The Sports Council's National Centre for Mountain Activities is at Plas-y-Brenin at Capel-Curig (06904) 394.

Plas Tan-y-Bwlch at Maentwrog (0766) 85324 is the Snowdonia National Park study centre offering day and residential courses about the countryside and conservation.

Theatr Gwynedd, at Bangor, encourages local Welsh and English productions and Oriel at Ffordd Gwynedd has an Arts For All programme.

# Clwyd Countryside and Heritage

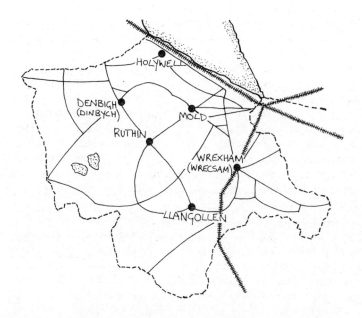

From the lowlands of the Dee to the Clwydian range and Berwyn mountains is a land that is rich in contrast and interest. Home to the mightiest of Welsh warrior princes, Owain Glyndŵr, it is for the most part as rich as he. Imaginative as he was in his challenge to unite a Welsh nation against an English throne, after years of struggle he eventually went into hiding in 1409 and in such a wild upland territory his whereabouts were always unknown.

This mainly sparsely populated upland area is dominated by hill farming of sheep on the slopes of the Berwyns, Mynydd Hiraethog and the Clwyd range, farming practice which has continued since ancient times for the area is littered with high hillforts and settlements dating from prehistoric ages. The exception is the Clocaenog Forest, a vast expanse of coniferous forest, but elsewhere in the valleys around Ruthin and Dinbych (Denbigh) mixed woodlands are more common. As is to be expected, land use in Clwyd is very much a reflection of the geology and climate. In these high hills, the Silurian and carboniferous rock beds have been eroded to wide moorland plateaux with shale outcrops. The resulting heather moorlands with marshy headstreams attract an array of upland wildlife and plants.

For many, however, the beauty of Clwyd lies in the limestone ridges such as the Clwyds covered in lime-loving plants – harebell, milwort and rock rose. The landscape is broken by the deeply incised rifts of the Clwyd, Dee, Ceiriog and Tanat, fast-flowing rivers squeezing through narrow passes to the lowlands of Shropshire or Clwyd. These valleys offer a varied habitat for wildlife with mixed farming, a still considerable cover of indigenous woodland host to woodpecker and flycatcher, and some herb-rich meadows. The Dee loops in horseshoe fashion through Wrecsam Maelor, an area of lowland, to its estuary – recognised internationally as a gathering place for thousands of waterfowl who tread patterns in the sand and mud.

Clwyd is very rural. The small towns and villages are still working rather than being wholly dormitory, except those within easy commuting distance of Chester. The Green traveller will more than likely head for Glyndŵr's Country, perhaps by way of Llangollen, home to the International Eisteddfod and probably the most popular destination in the region. Beyond is the small market town of Corwen which can also be reached by way of Dinbych (Denbigh), Ruthin or Mold. These towns are soaked in history, offer a good place to rest and allow relatively easy access to nearby countryside walking. The settlements become smaller and more sparse as you move west and public transport becomes erratic between Corwen and Pentrefoelas and on to Llanwrst.

There is another side to Clwyd. The lower, more gentle farming landscape in the Welsh borderlands around Chirk and the quiet villages of Wrecsam Maelor is very pleasant. Wrecsam, like the Dee Estuary, is more industrial. The coalpits have gone and the industrial heritage of the area is reflected at Bersham. Wrecsam is also a major shopping and communications centre. Those who seek very quiet areas should head for the Tanat Valley, an area of outstanding beauty where the pace is slow and villages have not changed much over the decades. This is after all the essence of rural Wales.

**Tourist information:** Halkyn Tourist Information Centre (0352) 780144; Llangollen Tourist Information Centre (0978) 860828; Mold Tourist Information Centre, Town Hall (0352) 59331; Pentrefoelas Heritage Village (06905) 343; Ruthin Tourist Information Centre, Craft Centre (08242) 3992; Wrecsam Tourist Information Centre, Memorial Hall (0978) 357845.

**Transport:** Fflint and Prestatyn are the main railway stations for those travelling to St. Asaph, Dinbych (Denbigh) and Holywell by bus. Wrecsam (Wrexham) is also served by rail, from Chester and Shrewsbury, as are Ruabon and Chirk. Wrecsam is an important centre for buses through to Glyndŵr country (i.e. Llangollen and Corwen), the Tanat valley and also to Wrecsam Maelor. Crosville Wales run most services but a number of independents have local services into the more sparsely populated areas. Bws Clwyd produces a route planner and timetables. Contact (0352) 2121 ext. 4035.

Glyndŵr Country is definitely for cycling. The use of mountain bikes is contentious but they are ideal for rugged back lanes and steep climbs. A useful port of call is The Mountain Bike Centre at Cilcain (0352) 740147 (Bws Clwyd B31). At Llangollen bikes (and canoes) can be hired at The Welsh Canal Holiday Centre (0978) 860702. There is also cycle hire at West End Cycles, Old Colwyn (0492) 518578.

Canoes can also be hired at Mile End Mill, Berwyn (0978) 861444 (but it is mainly a coaching centre). Wild Wales Walks (0490) 2226, based at Cynwyd near Corwen (Crosville Wales 94), arrange excellent guided walking holidays in this part of Wales and offer wholesome food.

**Access to the countryside:** Walking in the area is good, with Offa's Dyke Path passing along the Clwydian range of hills and paths being improved in some parts of Clwyd. The work of the Ramblers Association in the area and particularly of member Gordon Emery has led to a series of superb little walks booklets being issued in a series known as 'Walks in Clwyd', which can be found in bookshops, libraries and Tourist Information Centres in the area as is *Walks Around Wrexham Maelor*. The Maelor Way, linking the Offa's Dyke

61

Path near Chirk to the Sandstone Trail at Grindley Brook has also been pioneered by the same author.

In the north-east of Clwyd is the Greenfield Valley Heritage Park near Holywell (Bws Clwyd A9, 47, 48, 52). Wepre Country Park and nearby Ewloe Castle, a twenty minute walk from Shotton railway station, is another popular local haunt. In the Wrecsam area the beautiful Erddig Hall (Bws Clwyd 2, 3, 4, 5) is surrounded by exquisite parkland. Six miles south, at Cefn Mawr (Bws Clwyd 2) is Tŷ Mawr Country Park. In Glyndŵr country are two key country parks, Loggerheads near Mold (Bws Clwyd B2, 14) and Moel Fammau (Bws Clwyd 76) a few miles away. A clear path joins the two.

In the Llangollen area, the Llangollen Canal provides horse-drawn boats and the steam railway offers trips up to Berwyn. Both offer access to the nearby countryside including walks to Valle Crucis Abbey and the Pillar of Eliseg thought to be a burial mound dating from a thousand years ago. Local guided walks can be arranged through the Tourist Information Office. Along the length of the Llangollen railway branch are superb walks, across the Pontcysylite Aquaduct, 120 feet above the River Dee, or through Chirk Tunnel and into the gorge of the Ceiriog Valley (Bws Clwyd BM60) overlooked by Chirk Castle. To the south lie the Tanat Valley and the Berwyn range of mountains offering great walks, but they are not all that clear on the ground. The short walk to Pistyll Rhaeadr, the highest waterfall in Wales, is a favourite of many local people. Further west are the visitor centre and nature trails at Clocaenog Forest beyond Ruthin, the visitor centres at Llyn Brenig and the Alwen Reservoir offering information, an archaeological trail and other self-guided routes.

**Museums:** The area contains a considerable number of ruined castles which reflect the continual struggle between the Welsh and English throughout the centuries – Dinbych, Dinas Bran, Fflint, Hawarden and Ruthin are all open to the public. One of the best local museums is the Daniel Owen Centre at Mold, illustrating the life of one of Wales' leading novelists in the last century. Mold also has a good self-guided town trail. St. Winefride's Chapel, Holywell houses a Holy Well which has attracted pilgrims for centuries. Just south of Wrecsam is the Bersham Industrial Heritage Museum on the site of John 'Iron Mad' Wilkinson's ironworks; this is also the start of the eight mile Clywedog Trail featuring the valley's industrial past. Another distinctly Welsh museum is the Ceiriog Memorial Institute in Glyn Ceiriog offering an insight into local history. It is a few miles from Chirk (Bws Clwyd 60, 61).

Plas Newydd at Llangollen, the one-time home of two eccentric aristocratic ladies, provides an insight into life in earlier times and the Canal Museum at Llangollen displays the history of canal navigation. Clwyd Archaeology Service run occasional daybreaks and voluntary digs (0352) 2121.

**Bookshops:** Y Siop Lyfrau, Upper Clwyd Street, Ruthin provides a huge selection of books and maps. The Bookstore in Vale Street, Dinbych (Denbigh) also has a selection of local interest.

**Craft workshops:** The Abakhan Mill Shop (0745) 560312 is worth a visit for the buildings alone, whereas the Tri Thŷ Centre near Mold (0352) 771 359 specialises in craft and needlework as well as supplying good food. The Ruthin Craft Centre (08242) 4774 and the Llangollen Craft Centre offer a wide range of locally-made goods. Llangedwyn Mill Craft Centre (0978) 861887 in the Tanat Valley (Bws Clwyd 79) includes local craftspeople working in the restored malt house. The working corn mill at Pentrefoelas is well worth a visit (Bws Clwyd 90).

**Wholefoods:** You can get good food from Simon's Wholefood Shop and Bakery in Corwen; Nettles Wholefood Shop and Restaurant, Vale Street, Dinbych (Denbigh); and vegetarian snacks at The Corn Exchange, Ruthin. Ann Owen Delicatessen in Love Lane, Dinbych sells several Welsh cheeses. Mold Health Stores, Ewl Road, Mold sells wholefoods. Good Taste in Market Street, Llangollen provides wholefoods as does Beanstalk Natural Foods, Central Arcade, Wrecsam. Buck Farm, Hanmer offers wholefood fare and bed and breakfast for vegetarians and vegans.

**Health:** Herbal Health, King Street, Wrecsam stocks medicinal products.

**Co-operatives:** Wheatsheaf Workshops in Wrecsam is a co-operative resource and advice centre (0978) 822599.

**Community initiatives:** Canopy is an action group concerned with peace, conservation and human rights matters. Details are available from local libraries.

Rhuddlan Town Conservation Society aims to conserve Rhuddlan and maintain local paths. Details can be obtained from the library.

There is a Welsh language centre, Canolfan Iaith, at Dinbych (Denbigh). Deiniol's Residential Library (0244) 532350 offers residential courses in academic subject areas.

The Llangollen International Musical Eisteddfod (0978) 860236 is the world's leading festival of choral music and folk song and dance.

The European Centre for Traditional and Regional Cultures at Castle Street, Llangollen has a number of interesting displays including aspects of Welsh culture.

# *Meirionnydd*

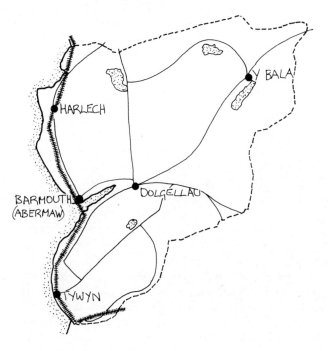

Two world famous nineteenth-century geologists, Sir Roderick Murchison and Adam Sedgwick, fought bitterly over the classification of the rocks lying beneath the landscape of Meirionnydd, the southern eroded dome of Snowdonia. The rocks date from Cambrian and Ordovician eras (600-400 million years BC) which makes them as old as most of North Wales. Like the mountain structure to the north, the remnants we see today were thrust up from the oceans during periods of intense earth movement and volcanic activity, with layering of intermediate sedimentary rocks laid down during the lengthy intervals between movements. Thus the harder rocks have remained as mountain peaks such as Arennig Fawr, Aran Fawddwy and Cader Idris. The inner dome comprises mainly Cambrian rocks as exposed in the Rhinog ridge down to Harlech.

Meirionnydd is therefore an area dominated by rugged mountains, boggy hollows, barren windswept moorland ridges broken by a major estuary, the Glaslyn, in the north and by a major rift valley in the south running through Bala and becoming exciting as it turns into the Mawddach Estuary and enters Cardigan Bay. In prehistoric times these hills were well-frequented by Celtic and earlier tribes living high above the rich coastal stretches of Dyffryn Ardudwy and Morfa Harlech, with burial chambers, cairns and small forts dating from both Bronze and Iron Ages.

Farming has continued as the main economic activity and much of the area is characterised by small fields enclosed by drystone walls, with woodland streams and gullies offering a retreat from fields now sown with rye grass. It is mainly an area of sheep farming, but in places Welsh black cattle are kept as they are particularly hardy. Some moorlands are retained for grouse shooting although the traditional black grouse has been in decline during this century mainly because of changing habitats. Coniferous forests do not provide the cover they seek and moves are afoot to create suitable new habitats.

The villages and towns of Meirionnydd are small and for the most part pleasant. Y Bala, on the edge of the very large natural lake Llyn Tegid, was once a stocking manufacturing town and became a major centre for the Welsh nonconformist church. It is a bustling place, being a major through route to the coast as well as a market town. The 94 bus passes through it and through dozens of villages on its scenic route from Wrecsam to Dolgellau and Abermaw (Barmouth), two very contrasting towns. The former is very much a Welsh market town providing some comforts for welcome visitors on their adventure to Cader Idris. The streets and squares are architecturally interesting with small shops of character and a real sense of identity. Abermaw, on the other hand, has long ceased to be a working port and is now very much dominated by the tourist trade, mainly from the Midlands. It splits into two towns, the narrow main street of some interest on one side of the railway track and the less pleasant car park cum amusement area on the other side before you reach the sands. The view of the Mawddach Estuary and mountains from the old harbour walls, however, is magnificent.

To the north lies Harlech, famous for its castle, its song and the cultural Coleg Harlech, a natural gateway to the Rhinog range. To the south is Tywyn with its little steam railway into the hills, and Aberdyfi, much more of a maritime community looking to the Dyfi estuary. Inland are the pockets which few visit: the romantic castle site of Castell-y-Bere, a delightful walk from Abergynolwyn; Corris and Aberllefenni with their slate mining tradition; Llanfachraeth beyond Foel Offrwm in the Dolgellau foothills where gold diggers once worked; and Dinas Mawwdwy where mining has now given way to farming once again.

Welsh culture is strong in Meirionnydd and chapels, eisteddfod-dau and markets are still very much a way of life for those who live and work here.

**Tourist information:** Aberdyfi Tourist Information Office (0654 72) 321; Bala Tourist Information Centre, High Street (0678) 520367; Dolgellau Tourist Information Centre, The Bridge (0341) 422888; Harlech Tourist Information Centre, High Street (0766) 780658; Tywyn Tourist Information Office, High Street (0654) 710070.

**Transport:** British Rail runs a service along the Cambrian Coast line between Machynlleth and Pwllheli which calls at some very remote request halts as well as the main stations of Aberdyfi, Tywyn, Abermaw (Barmouth) and Harlech. The enquiry number is (0970) 612377. Crosville Wales is the main bus company in the area and they publicise routes alongside Bws Gwynedd in a promotional and a timetable leaflet available from local Tourist Information Offices. The Dyfi Sherpa is a co-ordinated summer package involving British Rail, Crosville Wales and the Talyllyn narrow gauge steam railway. An all-in ticket lets you ride a triangle between Machynlleth and Tywyn through magnificent scenery on bus, steam and diesel. There are a number of amazing bus services passing through remote areas, so why not try the Thursdays-only market bus from Bala up to Llŷn Celyn or the Dolgellau to Llanfachraeth buses for a distinctly different rural ride?

Cycling in the area is not particularly pleasant on the main roads, but keep off the beaten track and Meirionnydd is yours. There is a cycle hire centre, the Mountain Bike Adventure, which offers in-struction and tours of Coed-y-Brenin forest; it is at Maesgwm Visitor Centre, near Dolgellau. See Montgomeryshire for details of cycle hire and holiday packages.

**Access to the countryside:** Walking in Meirionnydd offers great variety. There are the magnificent climbs around Cader Idris from Dolgellau or up on Rhinog Fawr near Harlech, challenges for the accomplished walker. At the same time there are dozens of local walks such as those written up in the booklet featuring walks from the Cambrian Railway, and in local leaflets highlighting high level walks such as the famous Precipice Walks above the Mawddach estuary or the town trail at Abermaw. The steam railways provide access to the countryside during the summer. The Rheilffordd Llyn Tegid (Bala Lake Railway) allows exploration of the lakeside at intermediate stations. The Fairbourne and Barmouth railway is ideal for a round trip, including a ferry crossing of the estuary, a ride on the steam railway, perhaps a visit to Butterfly Safari, then a return walk or journey on the British Rail Cambrian Coast line. The Talyllyn railway from Tywyn to Nant Gwernol offers superb short walks around the Dolgoch Falls and above Abergynolwyn. This area is involved in the Festival of the Countryside, see page 10 for details.

In the north of Meirionnydd there are woodland trails around the Snowdonia National Park Study Centre (076685) 324 at Plas Tan-y-Bwlch, Maentwrog (Bws Gwynedd 1, 2, 38). There is a chance to go rafting at the National White Water Centre (0678) 520826 near Y Bala (Bws Gwynedd 69, Thursdays only), or to try other water sports or mountain bike hire at Stan Cooper's, High Street, Bala (0678) 521059 (Bws Gwynedd 94). There is an open farm at Cyffdy near Bala and several woodland walks in Coed-y-Brenin Forest from the Maesgwm Forest Visitor Centre (Bws Gwynedd routes 2, 35).

Along the coast there are walks around Harlech (train or Bws Gwynedd 38) including the Snowdonia National Park 'Branwen's Walk' and longer rambles up to Nant Col, Cwm Bychan and the Roman Steps, a set of causeway stones said to be of Roman origin but more likely to have been a packhorse way. A short distance south is a beachcomber's paradise at Llandnwg (train) where an ancient church lies covered in the sand dunes. Another lovely walk is along the Mawddach estuary to Penmaenpool, where there is a nature information centre in the old railway signal box (Morfa Mawddach, by train). North of Aberdyfi is Trefrifawr working farm (065472) 247 standing high above the Dyfi estuary.

In the Dolgellau area are several local walks, the Precipice Walks, Cymmer Abbey, Glyn Arran and the Torrent Walk near Brithdir. To

68

the south at Aberllefenni (Bws Gwynedd 34) are a number of woodland trails from the Foel Friog picnic site.

**Museums:** Harlech Castle is a magnificent structure built by Edward I. Further south are slate caverns at Llanfair (Bws Gwynedd 38) and in Barmouth there is a lifeboat museum by the quayside. Clogau St. David's Gold Mine (0341) 422026 offers a fascinating insight into the only working gold mine in the UK and the entry price includes transport from Dolgellau (check for details at the Tourist Information Office). The Railway Museum at Corris (Bws Gwynedd 2, 34) tells the story of this isolated narrow gauge railway serving the slate quarries.

**Bookshops:** Awen Meirion in Y Bala stocks a good number of Welsh books.

**Craft workshops:** The Maes Artro Craft Village at Llanbedr (train) is a community of local craftspeople. The Corris Craft Centre (Bws Gwynedd 2, 34, 59) is a recently created 'village' of craftspeople producing a wide range of goods. There is also the Corris Pottery which produces a range of ware capturing aspects of the local scenery. The Meirion Woollen Mill at Dinas Mawddwy has re-used the old engine shed of the railway line that once served this small town when mining was its primary occupation.

**Organic initiative:** The organic nursery at Tŷ Nant, Gelliydan, near Maentwrog sells a selection of organically grown trees and shrubs.

**Wholefoods:** The Old Rectory at Maentwrog is a well-known restaurant serving a selection of vegetarian dishes. Lawrenny Lodge at Barmouth prepares vegetarian meals. The Old Station Coffee Shop in Dinas Mawddwy provides really lovely wholesome food. Dylanwad Da in Dolgellau also offers a good range of vegetarian dishes and the Tyddyn Llan Hotel, Llandrillo, near Bala offers good food in a congenial atmosphere. Rosey's Wholefoods in Tywyn sells a range of wholefoods.

**Energy:** The Ffestiniog hydro-electric power station at Tan-y-Grisau has a visitor centre (0766) 830465 ext. 40, as does the more controversial Trawsfynydd nuclear power station nearby.

**Community initiatives:** The RSPB at Penmaenpool has done a considerable amount of work to encourage people to conserve the local environment.

69

# Ceredigion

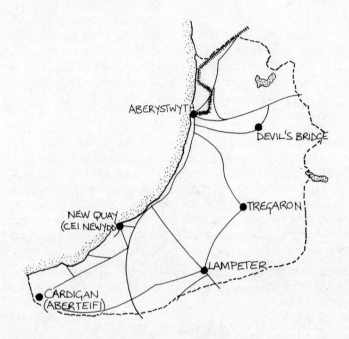

Ceredigion, lying between the Dyfi and Teifi rivers and bounded by the great Plynlimon range and the mountainous plateaux of Esgair Hir, Llethr Llwyd, Mynydd Pencarreg and Brechfa which make up the Cambrian range, is a land of promise. At one time known as the Green Desert, a reflection of the vast expanses devoted to sheep and dairying, farmers are now looking to all manner of diversification in order to make ends meet and newcomers have moved in to set up new businesses. They are very often in tune with the environment, perhaps woodworkers and spinners or weavers seeking to make a living in peaceful surroundings.

Once off the hills that lie to the east, it is a gently undulating land fed by stream and river bound by a magnificent stretch of coast that deserves to be cherished. The coast headlands and cliffs from north of Aberystwyth to Aberteifi (Cardigan) give way to sand and shingle beaches and narrow estuaries. Like other stretches of Welsh coastline, it has been designated a Heritage Coast and if these words are to mean anything there must be a continuous endeavour to stop pollution from killing wildlife in Cardigan Bay and to make every beach of Blue Flag standard so that children may play in safety.

As in other parts of Mid Wales agriculture dominates, although massive forests and reservoirs have removed much of the traditional sheep rearing on mountain ranges. Tourism has increased considerably during the past decade, but not to anywhere near the levels of South Pembrokeshire. The coastal resorts seem to attract the majority of visitors and the flow of traffic cloggs the coastal route at peak summer times so much that Aberteifi (Cardigan) becomes gridlocked and residents pray daily for the completion of the by-pass.

Wildlife is rich in Ceredigion and there are unusual features such as the bog Cors Caron near Tregaron, rimmed by moor grass and heathers, with wetter areas and small pools being covered in mosses, light scrub, sedge and wet-seeking plants such as bog asphodel and sundew. Coot and mallard, snipes and warblers are some of the birds readily spotted. There is limited access here, but none to Cors Fochno (Borth Bog), a very large bog indeed and a site of considerable importance so access is restricted to permit holders.

Another interesting feature is the rich wildlife in the upper reaches of the Ystwyth and most of the Teifi, including the European otter now found in the latter thanks to the work of the Otter Haven Project. Apart from the rivers there is a distinct lack of the freshwater pools and flowering meadows found in other parts of Mid Wales.

Most of Ceredigion's settlements are on the coast, from the small seaside locations of Borth, Aberaeron, Aberporth and Cei Newydd (New Quay) each with its own identity to the market towns of Aberteifi (Cardigan), Tregaron and Llandysul, of which the first is the most important. Lampeter, of course, is a market centre, but it also has an important role as a university town, as does Aberystwyth. They are both centres of culture and are distinctly Green. Of all Wales there is more going on here to raise awareness about Green issues than anywhere else in the country. Aberystwyth is also an ideal place from which to tour into wilder parts as the networks of road, rail or bus radiate from the town.

Move away from the coast and Ceredigion is full of winding lanes between towns and villages. A fine way to spend a week is to potter about them on bicycle, chancing upon mills and workshops, farm-house dairies and old pubs nestled in the back streets of the market towns. This is part of the old Wales, an experience not to be missed, a glimpse of rural life at a civilised pace.

**Tourist information:** Aberaeron Tourist Information Centre, The Quay (0545) 570602; Aberystwyth Tourist Information Centre, Terrace Road (0970) 612125; Aberteifi (Cardigan) Tourist Information Centre (0239) 613230; Lampeter Tourist Information Office, Town Hall (0570) 422426; Cei Newydd (New Quay) Tourist Information Office, Church Street (0545) 560865; Tregaron Tourist Information Office, District Council Offices, Dewi Road (09744) 248.

**Transport:** British Rail runs into Borth and Aberystwyth from Shrewsbury. Aberystwyth is the main railhead for the north of the area, but Caerfyrddin (Carmarthen) in the south also offers good connections. There are through bus services from Caerfyrddin (Carmarthen) railway station to Aberteifi (Cardigan) and Richards provides a service from Caerfyrddin (Carmarthen) bus station to Lampeter. The bus network between towns and along the coast is fine for travelling between the main centres, but there are fewer buses to isolated places such as Ponterwyd or Tregaron. Crosville Wales is the main company in the area. Dyfed County Council provides a route planner which is available from tourist information outlets, as are summary timetables.

Surprisingly there are few cycle hire centres in Ceredigion. There is Red Dragon Cycle Hire at Borth (0970) 84397, but to our knowledge no others exist at present. There ought to be, for there are miles and miles of quiet back lanes linking villages and craft centres, working farms and mills, making a week's holiday touring the area a dream.

**Access to the countryside:** Ceredigion takes its walking seriously. There are packs of twenty-five walks based in the Aberystwyth area as well as twenty-one walks along the Ceredigion coast and walks around Cardigan and the Teifi Valley. The Heritage Coast Service arranges a summer programme of guided walks and talks featuring the coastline. Dyfed County Council produces a series of

'County Walks' leaflets including Lampeter, Strata Florida and Devil's Bridge.

North of Aberystwyth is the RSPB Ynyshir Visitor Centre, near Glyndyfi (065) 474 265 (Bws Gwynedd route 2), and nearby is the Ynyslas Wildlife Information Centre (0970) 871640 with nature trails and bookshop (Crosville Wales routes 511, 512, 520, 524 or train to Borth). In the vicinity is Borth Livestock Centre (0970) 871224. At Dihewdis a rare breeds working smallholding is open at Rhyd-y-Cwrt Farm (0570) 470333.

East of Aberystwyth is the Vale of Rheidol and what better way to enjoy the scenery than by taking the narrow gauge steam railway to Devil's Bridge. There is a charge to see the falls here, but they are so beautiful it is worth it. Just south is the Arch Forest Trail through historic woodland. Near Ponterwyd is the Bwlch Nant Yr Arian Forest Centre with trails and rambles (Crosville Wales 501) and PowerGen at Cwmrheidol offers tours of the hydro-electric power station and a walk around their nature trail (nearest bus Crosville 501). In Aberystwyth itself there are fine walks around the harbour and also on the summit of Constitution Hill, served by an electric cliff railway.

South of Aberystwyth off the road to Tregaron near Llanafan is a forest walk leading to several Iron Age hill forts and also to a haven for butterflies. A leaflet is available from the Ystwyth Forest Office at Llanafan. The nearest bus is the Crosville Wales 562-568. There are of course superb longer hikes across the drovers roads from Strata Florida and Tregaron to the Heart of Wales; Hillscape at Blaen-y-ddol, Pontrhydygroes (097422) 640 offer walking packages in the area. There is a nature trail into Cors Caron National Reserve from a car park near Maesllyn Farm on the Pontrhydygroes to Tregaron road. Also near Tregaron is the Brimstone Wildlife Centre (097423) 439 at Penuwch. At Capel Cynon, Bryn Cerdin Farm (023 975) 371 welcomes visitors and sells produce such as milk and free range eggs. The National Trust's Mwnt Cliff with beach and ancient white-washed church has magnificent views but is a good four or five miles' walk from Aberteifi (Cardigan).

**Museums:** North of Aberystwyth is the Dyfi Furnace at Egl-wysfach (Crosville Wales 2), a charcoal-fired furnace where iron ore was smelted during the eighteenth century. At the same time a visit to the nearby Hen Efail, a restaurant serving good wholefood and

73

adjacent craft centre, is worthwhile as is a local walk in Artists Valley, so named because of its attraction for artists.

East of Aberystwyth is the Llywernog silver-lead mine (0970) 85620 with good displays on lead mining in Ceredigion, water power and the miner's way of life (Crosville Wales 501).

In Aberystwyth itself the Ceredigion Museum in Terrace Road houses a number of exhibitions in an old music hall which in some respects is interesting. There is also a museum, Aberystwyth Yesterday, at the railway station. The recreated Victorian Camera Obscura on Constitution Hill is most unusual, as are the views it offers of Aberystwyth.

To the south are the ruins of Strata Florida Abbey near Tregaron, one-time centre of Welsh literature (Crosville Wales 562-568). Near Aberteifi (Cardigan) is the medieval fortress of Cilgerran Castle (Crosville Wales 400). The Maesllyn Woollen Mill Museum (023975) 251 illustrates the changes from hand spinning and weaving to power-driven machinery. In Aberteifi (Cardigan) is a small local history museum at the Council Offices, Morgan Street.

**Bookshops:** A.B.C. Bookshop in Bridge Street, Lampeter has a local stock. In Aberystwyth there are a few bookshops specialising in Welsh books including Siop y Pethe, Galloway Booksellers and Ystwyth Books.

**Craft workshops:** Ceredigion has a thriving craft industry producing all manner of goods. We cannot do justice to them all but have attempted to list those where people work on the premises and welcome visitors:

Ystwyth Wood Products (097422) 349 at Pantlldiart, Brynafan not far from Pontrhydygroes (nearest bus Crosville Wales 562-568) makes a range of turned wood items. Castell Flemish (097421) 639, near Tregaron (Crosville Wales 515/516) produces handthrown and decorated stoneware. In Tregaron itself is Canolfan Aur Cymru (the Welsh Gold Centre), licensed users of Welsh gold and makers of exclusive Celtic design jewellery (Crosville Wales 515/516). Near Lampeter is Silverweed at Post Office House, Cwmann (0570) 423254 which offers courses in jewellery design using precious stones (nearest regular bus, Lampeter). Not far from Lampeter at Llanwnnen is Felin Yr Aber mill (0570) 480956 set within a small farm (Davies Route 202).

At Llanarth Pottery (Crosville Wales 550) you can see the potter turning fine domestic stoneware. At Cilcennin furniture maker Andrew Cotterhill (0570) 470120 uses hardwoods. Chapel Crafts (0239) 810866 at Aberporth (Richards/Crosville 550) is a marketing co-operative of local craftspeople and many demonstrate their working skills at the centre. On the road to Aberteifi (Cardigan) is Castle Crafts (0239) 654405, mainly a woodcraft workshop and shop.

In the south of Ceredigion are the Curlew Weavers (023975) 357, textile manufacturers, at Rhydlewis (Route 444, very infrequent). Just south of Llandysul is Brambles at Bancyfford (055 932) 2665, where handmade patchwork in traditional patterns can be seen. Also near Llandysul is Rock Mill, Capel Dewi (055932) 2356, spinners and weavers. At Cenarth is a seventeenth-century working flour mill and coracle centre (0239) 710209 where you can see how coracles are made (Davies 460, 461). Nearby in Lechryd is the David Beattie studio (0239) 87649, where the ancient craft of etching is practised (Davies 460, 461).

**Organic initiative:** A visit to Brynllys organic farm at Dolybont (Crosville Wales 520, 524) is a must. This farm has been farmed on an organic basis for generations and organic produce can be bought from Rachel's Dairy.

**Wholefoods:** In Aberystwyth is Maeth y Meysydd, Princes Street, selling organically-grown food and environmentally-friendly products. The Windsor Health Centre sells a range of goods and Frost Fresh in the Market Hall specialises in organic and local fresh produce. The latter also runs the Salad Shop in Great Darkgate Street, a real food takeaway. Ceredigion Wholemake on Llanbadarn Road are specialist bakers of organic bread and vegetarian and vegan foods. The Fountain Inn at Trefechan, near Aberystwyth, offers home made vegetarian and vegan food. At Dolybont, near Borth, Rachel's Dairy (see above) sells a wide range of organically-grown produce.

At Tregaron Sue's Wholefoods is on Station Road. At Aberaeron a visit to The Hive on The Quay is essential to see how honey is made and to taste a range of delicious products. There is also a honey farm at Llawhaden. Netti's Vegetarian Wholefood can be found at the rear of the Railway Hotel, Lampeter on Thursdays and Fridays. The Mulberry Bush, Bridge Street, Lampeter sells vegetarian and vegan wholefoods as well as holistic and herbal remedies.

75

There has been something of a mini-revolution recently in Ceredigion when it comes to the production of good food. Merlin Cheddar is produced at Tyn-y-Llwyn, Pontrhydygroes; Acorn Ewes Cheese is made at Mesen Fach, Llanon; and Porthriw Dairy near Tregaron demonstrates the art of cheese making. At Maesllyn, Felin Gernos Dairy also makes farmhouse cheese and so does Geotre Isaf at Derry Ormond near Lampeter on an organic dairy farm. Teifi farmhouse cheese is made at Glynhynod Farm, Ffostrafol near Llandysul; and at nearby Rhydlewis butter making is demonstrated at Pant-yr-Holiad Garden.

Further south, Felin Geri, Cwm Cou (nearest bus Davies Bros 460-462) is a sixteenth-century mill grinding flour, where delicious wholesome food is baked to be served in a superb restaurant which specialises in Japanese food. The cafe at Theatr Mwldan, Aberteifi serves good food snacks and there are a number of shops selling wholefoods or Welsh farmhouse cheeses such as Go Mango in Black Lion Mews, Deli Delights and Trevor Andrews Delicatessen. Body Matters in Pendre sells cruelty-free beauty products. Aberteifi indoor market is worth a visit for local organic foods and cheeses. The impressive looking Granary, alongside the Teifi, is a wholefood specialist.

The Greens at Abercari near Cwm Cou (0239) 710250 offer bed and breakfast for vegetarian guests and also paint wildlife and natural subjects.

**Health:** Aromatherapy treatment is available by contacting (097423) 432.

**Co-operatives:** Marged Women's Shoes at Lampeter manufacture handcrafted boots and shoes.

**Community initiatives:** Ceredigion is indeed a very fertile place, being a centre for Green activity and having a strong Welsh cultural input. The excellent magazine *Y Ffynnon* (The Well) is produced by a group of volunteers, a well-written magazine highlighting Green and cultural matters as they affect this part of Wales.

Cymru Werdd (Green Wales) is produced by the Green Party, Trewelyan, Fford Bryn Y Mor, Aberystwyth SY23 2HX (0970) 625143, where enquiries regarding the party and its policies can be made.

There is a strong Friends of the Earth base in Aberystwyth (0970) 871354, and also at Lampeter, where contact can be made through The Mulberry Bush, Bridge Street.

Friends of Cardigan Bay, an organisation created by the efforts of Greenpeace and Friends of the Earth, aims to raise awareness about the gross pollution of Cardigan Bay and how matters can be improved for wildlife and humans. One of the major worries is the decline in populations of cetaceans such as dolphins and porpoises; hence the setting up of a Dolphin Watch volunteer group. Contact Nant y Deri, Llandre, Aberystwyth. Steps are being taken to establish a wider forum to safeguard the future of the bay.

The Local Jigsaw Campaign encourages local community councils and amenity groups such as Merched Y Mawr (Welsh Language) and Tai Cymru (Housing for Wales) to gather information about their own communities, appraise themselves and establish policies, campaigns and action plans to improve matters. The fundamental point is local control. The co-ordinator is based at the Rural Surveys Research Unit, Geography Department, University College of Wales, Aberystwyth.

Dyfed Wildlife Group is part of the Montgomery Wildlife Trust – see Montgomeryshire. There is a wildlife hospital near Cei Newydd (New Quay) (0545) 560462 which encourages community involvement and provides guided tours at certain times.

The Canolfan y Gelfyddydau (Arts Centre) at Aberystwyth (0970) 623232 offers a wide range of entertainment. The Aberteifi and Lampeter group of the Ramblers Association campaigns for improved local footpaths and participates in the Mid Wales Festival of the Countryside.

# Montgomeryshire

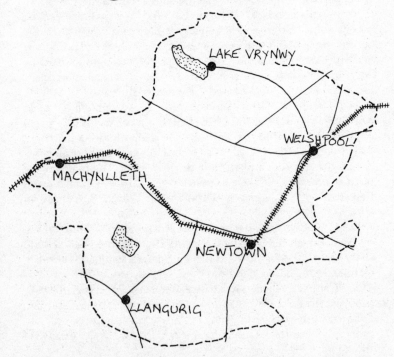

Stretching from the tidal reaches of the Dyfi estuary to the Marcher lands of Shropshire, Montgomeryshire (Maldwyn in Welsh) is a mixture of stark uplands and lush green river valleys, with the Wye, Severn and Vrynwy flowing eastwards to England. To the north it is bounded by the Berwyns, the last great hill range of North Wales consisting mainly of Silurian mud and slates. The gentler foothills give way to the wide valley of the Severn beyond Welshpool and westward to the slopes of Plynlimon, a landscape smoothed by glacial and post-glacial activity.

The Severn is a divider. To the north, in the Banwy and Vrynwy Valleys little has changed over the centuries. Prehistoric settlers used these natural routes but established their homes on high ground at

Carnedd Das, Eithen Clawdd Mawr, Dolanog, and Ffynon Arthur. Since medieval times the pastoral economy of the area has not changed; hill farming remains the prime occupation and even now little or no manufacturing industry exists in the area.

The Severn Valley in contrast reflects the rich cover of woodland of previous centuries, giving a tradition of timber-framed buildings and wooden belfries on the churches. This part of Montgomeryshire has also witnessed more industrialisation, with quarrying in Llanmynech and textile manufacture in centres such as Llanidloes, Newtown and their surrounding villages.

There is clearly more mixed woodland, particularly sessile oak, in and around the Severn than elsewhere, but the uplands have increasingly been sown with young conifers. The peaty upland areas attract birds such as merlin, plover and dunlin as well as other birds of prey. The river valleys, where in places kingfishers and dippers can be seen and, if you are fortunate, otters, are much more varied except where intensive cultivation occurs in the lower valleys.

The towns and villages are dispersed, as is the human population which must be outnumbered ten to one by sheep. In the north the main settlement is Llanfyllin, a charming market town renowned for being a malting town in earlier years, and nearby is the new village of Llanwddyn, the old one having been submerged in the massive Llyn Efyrnwy. Further south is Llanfair Caereinion by the Banwy, served by a remarkable survivor, the Llanfair and Caereinion Railway, originally closed to passengers in 1931, yet still steaming for the best part of the year in the 1990s.

Montgomery, nestled beneath its brooding castle, is a Georgian town of character, as are Llanidloes and Caersws; all are worthy of a visit. Welshpool, Newtown and Machynlleth lie on the rail route to the coast. Welshpool, with its magnificent station and canal heritage, nearby Powis Castle and local walks is bound to attract the Green traveller. Newtown, once home to Utopian Robert Owen, will also draw you; but it is to Machynlleth that most will go to visit the site of Owain Glyndŵr's 1404 Parliament and the nearby Centre for Alternative Technology.

**Tourist information:** Llanidloes Tourist Information Office, Longbridge Street (05512) 2605; Llanfyllin Tourist Information Office, Council Offices (069184) 8868; Machynlleth Tourist Information Office (0654) 702401; Newtown Tourist Information Office, Central Car Park (0686) 625580; Welshpool Tourist Information

Office, Vicarage Garden Car Park (0938) 552043.

**Transport:** British Rail's Cambrian line runs from Shrewsbury with stops at Welshpool, Newtown, Caersws and Machynlleth. Bus services in the area are variable, so plan your outings with care. The main towns and some key villages have a service Monday to Saturday, but the routes are very much determined by local market days. One way to find out about local communities is to catch the market day bus. Crosville Wales is the main company but there are several long-established independents such as Worthen Motors or Mid Wales Motorways who provide some of the services. Apart from the trains, public transport in the evening and on Sundays is virtually non-existent. The post buses around Llanidloes and Machynlleth, however, make for a completely different afternoon outing, calling at some of the remotest hamlets in Wales. All Tourist Information offices and libraries have public transport timetable information at hand.

Cycling activity is on the increase and the major cycle hire centre for the area is Joyrides (0654) 703109 by Machynlleth railway station. They also arrange self-guided package breaks.

**Access to the countryside:** In the northern section of Montgomery are a number of nature trails from the Visitor Centre at Llanwddyn by Lake Vrynwy, a reservoir built in the last century. There is also a trail around Tynygarreg Farm. One of the 'Self Guided Walks' series produced as part of the Festival of the Countryside is based around Llanfyllin (served by Llansilan Motor Services from Oswestry), where there is also a Bird and Butterfly World. Meifod, between Llanfyllin and Llanfair Caereinion has produced its own village trail with a superb insight into community life over the ages and the leaflet is available from local shops, pub and garage. There are other walks based in and around the Welshpool and Llanfair railway, a lovely one being at Ty'n Llan Farm, Castle Caereinion illustrating the work of a farm in Mid Wales. Another delightful walk is between Pont Llogel and Dolanog, researched by Llanfihangel Community Council and reflecting on the work of Ann Griffiths, a famous Welsh hymn writer who lived from 1776 to 1805. The Moors Collection of rare breeds near Welshpool is worth a visit.

The Montgomery branch of the Shropshire Union Canal also allows for short walks along the canal and Montgomery Cruises (0938) 553271 at Welshpool offers narrow-boat trips as well as hiring canoes and other boats. The canal is a haven for wildlife. There are self-guided trails near the canal at Berriew (Crosville Wales D75) and at Dolforwyn Castle (Crosville Wales D75) courtesy of the local landowners. Near Newtown is Fronlas Farm Nature Trail, set in delightful foothills.

There are three long-distance paths in the area. Offa's Dyke Path passes through Welshpool and on to Montgomery (Worthen Motors). Glyndŵr's Way is a circular path through very hilly country between Machynlleth and Knighton. The most recent path is the Dyfi Valley Way, a 108 mile circular route from Aberdyfi to Llanwchllyn by way of Corris and Dinas Mawddwy, returning via Mallwyd and Machynlleth to Borth and completing the circuit by the summer ferry from Ynys Las to Aberdyfi. The author of the accompanying book, Laurence Main, is a keen rambler who lives near Dinas Mawddwy and has written several books and booklets about walking in Mid Wales which are available generally. The Wynnstay Arms in Machynlleth offers walking packages with Laurence Main as walk leader. South of Machynlleth are walks around Llyn Clywedog (postbus from Llanidloes) and the Bryn Trail lead mine area. Not too far away is the Glaslyn Nature Reserve on the Plynlimon uplands (nearest postbus from Llanidloes to Dylife), a place if ever there was to replenish the spirit. Welshwalks based at Talbontdrain Guest House, Uwchygarreg, Machynlleth (0654) 702192 offer special walks packages particularly featuring wildlife interest.

Several of the Montgomeryshire Wildlife Trust Nature Reserves are open to the public, including Roundton Hill near Churchstoke, Glaslyn near Dylife (postbus from Llanidloes), Coed Pendugwm near Pentrobert, Cwm y Wydden near Dinnant and Severn Pond (Crosville Wales D71, D75), Welshpool.

**Museums:** Powis Castle (National Trust), a short walk from Welshpool, has a range of historical displays. In the town itself is the Powysland Museum at the Montgomery Canal Centre. The castle at Montgomery stands over the town and the Old Bell Museum recalls the history of the place, as does a self-guided leaflet prepared by the local Civic Trust. At Newtown are the Newtown Textile Museum illustrating the history of the Welsh cloth flannel industry, the Robert Owen Museum telling the remarkable story of this great social reformer, and the W.H. Smith shop and museum, the shop being a restoration of the original dating from 1927. To the south is the Llanidloes Museum at Llanidloes Market Hall (Crosville Wales

D75), one of several half-timbered buildings in the town. Machynlleth, Montgomery, Llanfyllin and Welshpool have historic town trail leaflets or booklets available.

In Machynlleth, the life of Owain Glyndŵr, the last native Prince of Wales and champion of an independent Wales in medieval times, is reconstructed in the restored Parliament House. The upper section of the building is now a Brass Rubbing Centre.

**Energy:** The Centre for Alternative Technology. The years of hard work and campaigning to establish a centre to research and illustrate alternative ways of living began to bear fruit in the 1970s. Since those early days Llwyngwern Quarry has been transformed into a major demonstration of alternative technology. This is a very broad term which the Centre defines to mean sustainable, fair, interdependent, non-destructive, pollution-free, cyclic and economical. The self-guided tour of the centre includes at every turn of the path practical demonstrations of biofuels, solar heating systems, water turbines, all manner of wind pumps and storage devices as well as an amazing organic garden packed with ideas to take home. The energy conservation house and other displays illustrate the way of life at the centre. With wholefood refreshment and a well-stocked bookshop, the Centre sends the visitor away enthused with ideas which can be applied to our everyday life. The Centre's next major project is to redevelop the site to address a wider range of topics and to build a cliff railway driven by water power. All this will require your support but this centre of international fame deserves it. Telephone (0654) 702400. Bws Gwynedd routes 2, 34 and 59 pass near the Centre (10 minutes walk) and it should really be a prime candidate for a walkway/cycle route from Machynlleth, as an alternative to taking a car.

**Bookshops:** Pethe Powys, Severn Street, Welshpool specialises in Welsh books but has a range of books in English on Wales. Dragon Books, Hall Street has a range of local books. In Newtown, the original W.H. Smith shop is in the High Street and local bookshop Griffiths and Griffiths is in Broad Street. Not Just Books in Great Oak Street, Llanidloes has a local selection, as does the Dyfi Valley Bookshop, Doll Street in Machynlleth which specialises in secondhand books. There is also The Bookshop in Hoel Maengwyn, Machynlleth and a specialist bookshop at the Centre for Alternative Technology.

**Craft workshops:** There are craft workshops at Lake Vrynwy, for example The Pottery at Foel Farm, Llansantffraid (0691) 828267. Hand-painted textiles are produced at The Plas Robin Chapel Workshop, Montgomery (Worthen Motors) and there is the Michael and Joanna Mosses Pottery at Llanbrynmair (Crosville Wales 522). Country Works Gallery at Sawmills, Kerry (0686 88) 434 displays a changing selection of country art and craftwork in a variety of media. In Welshpool, the main Welsh craft shop is Prentice Traders, and also in the town is the most unusual Makers (0938) 555014, a craft workshop where people can learn to paint, do pottery, or create with wool or yarn. They have a creche and coffee shop. At Berriew (Crosville Wales D75) Silver Scenes specialises in individual silver and pewter designs depicting nature. Ian Snow at Newtown and Llanidloes sells a range of craft products which fit into an ecologically sustainable category.

Machynlleth and surrounding area are a hive of activity. At nearby Penegoes (Crosville Wales 522) is the Felin Crewi Working Water Mill (0654) 3113, showing the work of the miller in a delightful location. The food at the cafe is good, as are the ground flour and the muesli. In Machynlleth itself the Glandwyryd Gallery produces ceramics and other crafts. In Eagles Yard are other workshops where Roger Whitfield produces furniture and Alison Morton makes colourful rag rugs, handwoven towels and other textiles. North of Machynlleth at Ceinws is Yr Oriel Fach Art Gallery (Bws Gwynedd routes 2, 34), which displays paintings mainly of Mid Wales countryside scenes.

**Wholefoods:** Seeds Restaurant in Llanfyllin serves wholesome food as does The Granary in Welshpool. The mill at Bacheldre, near Montgomery produces stoneground flour. In Newtown, Jay's Restaurant, Bank Tea Rooms and The Courtyard also produce wholefood dishes. Macbean in the High Street sells a range of products. Fron Haul, Llandinam is recognised for its vegetarian dishes. To the south, try Natural Foods, which is a co-operative, at Llanidloes. Amazingly, there is a vegetarian tea room, Llys Arwel, at Staylittle (postbus).

In Machynlleth, the Quarry Shop serves good wholefood meals, not surprisingly since it is a sister-enterprise to the cafe at the Centre for Alternative Technology. Speake's Delicatessen sells a good range of Welsh farmhouse cheeses.

**Health:** An interesting book, available locally, is *Welsh Herbal Medicine* by D. Hoffmann (Abercastle). The Dolafon Natural Healing Centre (068688) 706 concentrates on healing the whole person.

**Co-operatives:** Antur Efyrnwy is a community co-operative engaged in encouraging economic development in Llanwddyn. Dulas Engineering, an off-shoot of the Centre for Alternative Technology, specialises in the design of renewable energy systems.

**Community initiatives:** The Festival of the Countryside is in many respects a community initiative, since so many local people, clubs and societies get together to make the programme so enjoyable for the resident and the visitor.

The Tabernacle Arts Centre in Machynlleth encourages local productions.

The Montgomeryshire Wildlife Trust (0686) 624751, 8 Severn Square, Newtown does great work in the area.

Fforiad, a company seeking to encourage the development of sustainable Welsh tourism can be contacted on (0654) 702119.

Theatre Scallywag, based at the Centre for Alternative Technology, aims to bring awareness of current environmental and cultural issues into schools through the medium of interactive theatre (0654) 702400.

The Play Resource Centre in Newtown re-uses harmless materials from industry suitable for play. Contact Replay on (0686) 622267.

# The Heart of Wales

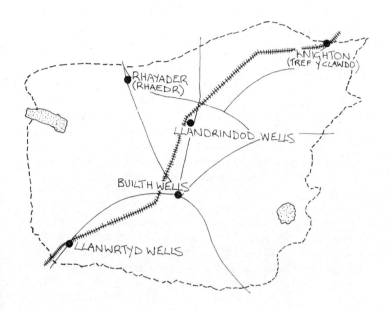

This part of the county of Powys, lying south of Montgomeryshire, stretching to the higher ground of the Cambrian mountains in the east and shielded by Radnor Forest and the Brecon beacons in the west is truly border country and has been witness to many bloody battles between the Welsh and the Norman Marcher lords. An earlier divide, Offa's Dyke, signifies the tension that remained for centuries, although trade still flourished and drovers roads are an important feature of the landscape.

Geologically, Mid Wales is similar to Montgomeryshire, with exposed shales and muds eroded to moorland plateaux and with softer sediments deposited in the valleys of the Wye and Lugg.

The Wye and its tributaries are important in terms of wildlife. From its peat bog source to the shallow rapids of Hay-on-Wye, this river provides a variety of habitats for wildlife despite increased pressures from modern farming practices. The remnants of woodland in its upper reaches are said to attract the rare red kite as well as the pied flycatcher and numerous warblers. The Wye is renowned for its salmon, although along with trout they are still considered to be declining in numbers.

Llandrindod Wells became famous a few years ago for its toad population which has a habit of mating in and around Llandrindod Lake. Hence the introduction of toad warning signs for motorists, who were not aware of this spring time phenomenon.

The economic mainstay of the area is hill farming and to a lesser degree quarrying. The population is sparse and villages and towns tend to be nestled around rivers and tributaries. In the north is the border town of Tref y Clawdd (Knighton) with its distinctive Victorian clock tower and market square. The area of Presteigne and New Radnor to the south is very quiet, and excellent walking and cycling territory for the Green traveller. Rhaedr (Rhayader) and Builth are market towns on the Wye, each having a very Welsh character and a focal point on market days. Llandrindod, Llangammarch and Llanwrtyd Wells developed principally as spa resorts during the last century. The legacy of taking the waters remains, so much so that Llandrindod in recent years has established a Victorian Festival which, while primarily commercial in intent, brings the community together with the visitor. The other two resorts are quieter, Llangammarch more so than Llanwrtyd, for the latter community really goes to town when it comes to special events. All are served by the British Rail Heart of Wales line and offer invigorating pastimes for the would-be traveller.

In many respects though the Welsh borderland is best reflected in the villages, in Old Radnor, Bleddfa, Glascwm, Abbeycwmhir and Llangunllo; places with often fewer than twenty or so houses, a chapel or church and a post office or pub. Visited by bike or bus, these ancient settlements unfold a rich history that gives meaning to the phrase used by the sixth-century poet Llywarch Hen – 'Powys, paradwys Cymru': Powys, the paradise of Wales.

**Tourist information:** Tourist Information Offices at Builth Wells, Croe Car Park (0982) 553307; Elan Valley Visitor Centre (0597) 810898; Tref y Clawdd (Knighton) Tourist Information

Office, The Old School (0547) 528753; Llandrindod Wells Tourist Information Office, Rock Spa Park (0597) 822600; Llanwrtyd Wells, The Bookshop (05913) 264; Presteigne, The Old Market Hall (0544) 260193; Rhaedr (Rhayader), The Old Swan (0597) 810591.

**Transport:** The British Rail Heart of Wales line is the main public transport lifeline in the area. Hotels and guest houses will pick you up from the local station, and people use the train to get from village to town and for trips to Shrewsbury and Swansea. It is very much a community railway. The main stations are at Knighton, Llandrindod Wells and Llanwrtyd Wells, but most trains will stop and pick up passengers at all halts on request so places like Garth or Dolau are easily reached. The biggest breakthrough in recent years has been the introduction of a Sunday 'Recreational Rambler' service with a morning train out of Swansea to Llandrindod, guided walks and a special connecting bus from Llandrindod to the Elan Valley. A free walks booklet is issued to those using the special train, which also calls at Sugar Loaf Summit halt between Cynghordy and Llanwrtyd Wells.

Buses tend to be infrequent and very much determined by schools and market day requirements. On Mondays they are all heading for Builth Wells, on Thursdays for Knighton, for example. The two main local companies, Cross Gates Motors and Roy Brown's Coaches serve most areas, but there are other independents. The hub of the network is Llandrindod Wells, right next to the railway station, so interchange is easy. Some of the runs are marvellous, such as the Tuesday and Saturday only route to Kington via New Radnor or the postbus to Abergwesyn. Timetable information is available from local libraries.

There is a cycle hire company at Rhaedr (Rhayader), Clive Powell (0597) 810585, specialising in mountain bike packages. Greenstiles Cycles, High Street, Llandrindod Wells (0597) 4594 also offers cycle hire. At Llanwrtyd Wells you will find the Red Kite Mountain Bike Centre at the Neuadd Arms (05913) 236. Bicycle Beano, based in Herefordshire, offers cycling packages in Mid Wales. Contact them on (0981) 251087.

**Access to the countryside:** There are three long-distance footpaths passing through the Heart of Wales – Offa's Dyke Path through Tref-y-Clawdd (Knighton), Old Radnor and on to Hay-on-Wye; the Wye Valley Way from Rhaedr (Rhayader) to Hay-on-Wye;

and Glyndŵr's Way. Local walks are published in and around Llandrindod Wells, particularly to the Radnorshire Trust's Bailey Einon wood; also at Llanwrtyd Wells (guided walks available in the summer); and to the Radnor Forest (from Dolau station or around the Elan or Claerwen valleys). The paths are difficult to follow elsewhere but matters are improving slowly. In the north of the area, the Offa's Dyke Heritage Centre (0547) 528753 offers ideas for getting out into the countryside.

Several walking packages are available in the area, all based near the Heart of Wales line. Hitch-n-Hike breaks are on offer from Willow Cottage, Tref y Clawdd (Knighton) (0547) 528060. Temewalks at Knucklas (0547) 520363 offer day walks, short breaks and week stays, as do Welsh Wayfaring Walks at Llanwrtyd Wells (05913) 236. Welsh Connections at Penybont (0597) 87476 (train) also provide walks and talks. Head for the Hills at Garth (05912) 388 organise great walking holidays. A self-guided package is available along Offa's Dyke from Welsh Wanderer, 6 George Street, Ferryhill, County Durham DL17 0DT (0740) 653169 but they also offer other Welsh breaks with guides.

A number of town trail leaflets or booklets are available from Tourist Information offices, some written by local people. The New Radnor leaflet describing the link of Sir George Cornewall Lewis, statesman and author, with the community of New Radnor (Cross Gates Motors) is fascinating. Start or finish at the very friendly Eagle Hotel. The leaflet featuring walks around Newbridge on Wye (Cross Gates or Roy Brown) and the Builth Wells town walk produced by Builth and District Heritage Society are also good.

The Welsh Sheeptacular (0597) 810898, at the Elan Valley Centre, allows an insight into Welsh sheep farming (Cross Gates Motors Wednesday and Sunday only or postbus). The Gigrin Farm Trail (0597) 810243 at Rhaedr (Cross Gates or Roy Brown or postbus) illustrates traditional farming and nature.

**Museums:** There is a small local history museum at Presteigne. At the Rock Spa at Llandrindod Wells you can also taste the waters, but beware not to take too much of the purgative! There is a local museum at Rhaedr.

**Bookshops:** Foreman's Emporium, Builth Wells sells local books, and the Offa's Dyke Heritage Centre at Knighton has a good range of outdoor books.

**Craft workshops:** The Bleddfa Trust at Bleddfa Old School Gallery (054781) 220 presents an interesting series of exhibitions (it's a lovely 4-5 mile walk from Llanbister Road station to Bleddfa and back). Jules Newman produces ceramics at Lower Esgair-Rhiw near Rhayader (0597) 810155; and the Marston Pottery (0597) 810875, also a short walk from Rhaedr, produces hand-thrown stoneware pottery. The Welsh Royal Crystal at Rhaedr (0597) 811005 makes and decorates full-lead Welsh crystal. Taylor's Woolcrafts (0982) 552403 at Builth Wells shows the making of handknitted woollen goods.

South of Builth, at Erwood old station is Woodgrain Crafts where a woodturner demonstrates craft skills. The Cambrian Factory just outside Llanwrtyd Wells (05913) 211 manufactures traditionally spun and woven Welsh wool.

**Wholefoods:** Van's Good Food Shop, Middleton Street, Llandrindod Wells, sells a range of organic wines, essential oils, etc. as well as wholefoods. Stredders at Llandrindod Wells specialises in vegetarian and vegan cuisine at their guest house. Castle Corner, Broad Street, Builth Wells, sells a selection of wholefoods.

**Health:** Llandrindod Wells grew up as a spa town and visitors can still take the waters at the Rock Spa.

**Co-operatives:** Artisan (0597) 824576 at Llandrindod Wells is a craft marketing co-operative. Owen Thomas Press Ltd. at Llandrindod Wells (0597) 823547 is a community project aiming to set up a working Victorian printing press as an attraction and to produce hand-printed items.

**Energy:** Practical Alternatives at Rhaedr (0597) 810929 has built up an innovative catalogue mainly of energy-saving devices and equipment.

**Community initiatives:** Gordon Green at the Neuadd Arms Hotel has for years been a driving force in introducing events to Llanwrtyd Wells which are open to resident and visitor alike, such as the Man Versus Horse Marathon, the World Bog Snorkling Championships and the Mid Wales Beer Festival!

The Wyeside Arts Centre at Builth Wells encourages local involvement.

Wales Vegan Group can be contacted at Bron Yr Ysgol, Parc Montpelier, Llandrindod Wells (0597) 823547.

The Radnorshire Wildlife Trust based in Llandrindod Wells can be contacted on (0597) 823298. The Llandrindod Wells Animal Sanctuary (0597) 824425 welcomes visitors to assist on a voluntary basis.

The Rail User Group for the Heart of Wales line have to be commended for getting local communities behind the line. Contact the Publicity Officer, HOWLTA, 38 High Street, Llanymddyfri, Dyfed SA20 0DD.

# Pembrokeshire

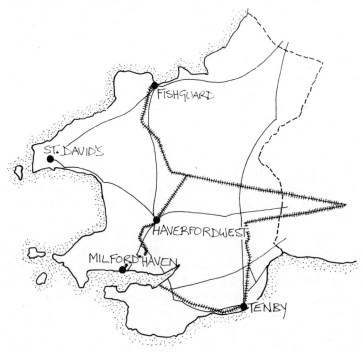

Mystical though Pembrokeshire may be, there are few areas of Wales that receive more visitors. It is the beauty of the coastline that appeals, an area designated a National Park, thus preventing the worst of the overdevelopment that has happened elsewhere. The varied nature of Pembrokeshire's scenery, both coastal and inland, with crags, vales, coves, sands and views is as memorable as any place on Earth. Add to this what can virtually be described as a re-birth of craft cottage industry and you begin to understand why the Green traveller might wish to come here.

The landscape reflects the jumbled nature of the geological strata beneath. Pembrokeshire contains some of the oldest rocks in Wales, with those of the Cambrian and pre-Cambrian eras, generally in the

91

north-west of the area, giving way to slightly younger Ordovician and Silurian beds towards the south coast of Dyfed. They do not, however, form dramatic peaks as one would expect, but are smoothed for the most part in a series of plateaux. Some of the steeply-cut valleys, such as the splendid Gwaun Valley, are most probably the effect of post-glacial activity although the Pembrokeshire landscape has not been affected greatly by ice sheets.

Wildlife is abundant. The coastline enjoys the company of grey seals, porpoises and dolphins and the variety of birds to be seen is probably greater than elsewhere in Wales. The offshore islands of Grassholm, Skokholm and Skomer have become something of a pilgrimage for naturalists from throughout Europe. The Cleddau estuary is home to wildfowl. Bosherton pools are also a refuge for waterfowl, and the nearby Stackpole cliffs are an important nesting site for all manner of birds. While agricultural practices have wiped out much wildlife in the Pembrokeshire interior the steeply-hedged lanes are still bedecked with a rich flora and the higher heathlands are covered in mat grass.

Prehistoric people have without doubt left their mark on this landscape. The concentration of remains in the Preseli Hills is impressive. Neolithic chambers, Bronze Age burial mounds, hut circles and Iron Age forts can all be found within a few miles. The bluestones used at Stonehenge came from Carn Menyn and it must have been an incredible feat to transport these huge stones to Salisbury Plain. The only way to appreciate these ancient sites, the menhirs and the mounds is to walk the hills at dawn or dusk with the sunlight slanting on these mysterious shapes.

Not that prehistoric sites are only to be found in the Preseli Hills. Pembrokeshire has numerous ancient monuments, from round barrows to cromlechs, castles and kilns. The old ports of Porthgain and Solva reflect a maritime heritage and of course Milford Haven with large oil tankers in the bay reminds us of the ever-present threat of immediate oil spill catastrophe; there have been incidents in recent years that have come close to it.

Pembrokeshire can be divided roughly into three areas as far as the Green traveller is concerned. First of all the coastal towns and resorts of Tenby and Saundersfoot, the busiest part and definitely for sun and sand seekers. Then we have the coastal villages and towns, each with its local beach or inlet harbour; they are the haunts of sailors and walkers of the coastal path. Finally there are the traditional towns of Pembroke, Narberth, Haverfordwest, St David's, Newport and Fishguard (although the latter is much more of a ferry port). They have not changed much over the years and offer interesting bases from which to investigate the labyrinth of lanes and hamlets where many craftspeople have settled. Wherever you stay, however, you are never far away from that irresistible coastline.

**Tourist information:** Fishguard Tourist Information Office, Hamilton Road (0348) 873484; Haverfordwest Tourist Information Office, High Street (0437) 763110; Kilgetty Tourist Information Office, Kingsmoor Common (0834) 813672; St. David's Tourist Information Office, City Hall (0437) 720392; Tenby Tourist Information Office, The Norton (0834) 2402.

**Transport:** British Rail lines run to Haverfordwest and Milford Haven, and a branch line runs from Whitland to Pembroke via Tenby. There is also a very limited service to Fishguard Harbour, two or three trains a day, to serve the boat to Eire. The bus network between Pembrokeshire towns is good and the Dyfed Route Planner available from Tourist Information Centres is invaluable. Some routes are particularly lovely, such as the route to St. David's or between Fishguard and Cardigan. Haverfordwest is a major interchange but it is possible to tour from Tenby or Fishguard.

Cycling is exhilarating when you move away from the busier beach areas and use the lanes between villages and towns. Cycle hire is available at Twr-y-Felin Outdoor Centre, near St. David's (0437) 720391. They also arrange activity breaks.

**Access to the countryside:** As it is partly in a National Park, the area is good for walking, particularly along the coast, despite the military use of land in places. The Pembroke National Park has a free publication *Coast to Coast* packed with ideas for getting into the countryside. It also issues a series of walks leaflets available locally.

In the north of Pembrokeshire, in the triangle between Fishguard, Narberth and Aberteifi (Cardigan), are miles and miles of back roads suitable for cycling away from it all, in particular the Gwaun Valley and a trail through the Preseli Hills between the prehistoric remains. At Felindre Farchog is Castell Henllys Iron Age Fort, an intriguing attempt to reconstruct life as it might have been in the Iron Age. Roundhouses, grain stores and animal shelters have been restored following excavations of the settlement and each summer further

93

digs are organised (Richards 412). Near Fishguard is Goodwick Moor, 38 acres of wetland managed by the Dyfed Wildlife Trust (Richards 410). Llys-y-Fran Reservoir, excavated to serve the Milford Haven oil refineries in 1971, has a $7^1/_2$ mile perimeter path and a nature trail. It lies to the north of Clarbeston Road station.

Heron's Brook (0834) 860723 near Narberth has a number of trails and a waterfowl centre. Nearby, Folly Working Dairy Farm (0834) 812731, open to the public most days, is a big hit with children. Colby Woodland Garden near Amroth (Silcox 351) has a number of fine walks. Manor House Wildlife and Leisure Park at St. Florence (Silcox 360) near Tenby has fine gardens and wooded grounds. Tenby Information Bureau has produced a book of local walks, including a town walk. A short walk from the town centre takes you to Silent World, an aquarium and wildlife art gallery set in an old chapel. Herberts Moor Open Farm (0646) 672532, Lamphey (train) has a number of nature and woodland trails.

In the south, St. David's Farm Park (0437) 721601 is a rare breeds survival centre (Richards 340, 411). Slebech Wood between Haverfordwest and Canaston has a trail; a Forestry Commission leaflet describes the woodland. Haroldston Wood, north of Broadhaven (Silcox 311) also has a self-guided trail leaflet. The National Trust arranges activity days such as orienteering and rocky pool searches at Stackpole (0646) 661359.

Offshore are islands such as Ramsey, home to seals and seabirds, sheep and deer. It is possible to take just a short trip but there are also guided walks and overnight accommodation can be arranged (0437) 781234. Skomer, Skokholm and Grassholm are well-loved by Green travellers and Dale Sailing (0646) 636349 organises trips to these spectacular islands. Dyfed Wildlife Trust offers accommodation and sometimes courses on the islands of Skomer and Skokholm. There's also a boat service from St. Martin's Haven to Skomer. From Tenby there are boat trips to the monastic retreat of Caldey Island.

**Museums:** According to tradition cottages like the Penrhos Traditional Welsh Cottage near Maenclochog were built overnight on common land and were known as 'Tŷ un nos' or the overnight house. Scolton Manor Museum, standing in a beautiful country park near Haverfordwest tells the story of Pembrokeshire rural life from prehistory to the present day. The Museum and Art Gallery in Haverfordwest, housed in the old gaol, has a mainly local emphasis with a touch of the military. There's a Maritime Museum at Milford

Haven and a Museum of Home at Pembroke. Selvedge Farm Museum (043 782) 264 at Clarbeston Road shows how farming has changed over the last ninety years. Picton Castle near Haverfordwest is home to the Graham Sutherland Art Gallery. The Leithyr Farm Museum (0437) 720245 at Whitesands Bay near St. David's contains a collection of farming equipment from earlier decades.

Black Pool Mill, Canaston Bridge near Narberth (09914) 233 is a restored partially water-driven mill from the last century (South Wales Transport 322). Amgueddfa Wilson (Wilson Museum), Market Square, Narberth, named after a local resident, is an unusual collection of Narberth bygones. The Tenby Museum which houses a local history collection is well worth a visit, as is the Tudor Merchants' House, a late fifteenth-century dwelling. The majestic castles of Tenby, Manorbier, Carew and Pembroke are open to the public. At Carew is also a restored tidal mill as well as the impressive Celtic cross.

## Bookshops:
In Newport, the Newport Bookshop, Market Street. In Fishguard, Seaways Books, West Street has a useful local collection. Bookmark in Quay Street, Haverfordwest sells Green books and magazines as well as recycled paper products. The Bookshop, Market Street also has a range of books on environmental matters. In Line at Tenby has a small Green section and the Pembroke Bookshop, Main Street, Pembroke is the main bookseller in that town.

## Craft workshops:
Pembrokeshire is home to many craftspeople making all sorts of lovely articles, very often in a traditional manner and using local resources wherever possible. We have attempted to list as many as possible from Aberteifi and Newcastle Emlyn southwards as some people might wish to get their bicycles out and plot a route down the lanes. Those listed usually demonstrate their skills and welcome visitors at any reasonable time. Many are in out-of-the-way places, so please telephone first to check that the workplace is open.

Welsh Willow Craft (0239) 613430 at Cippyn near St. Dogmaels (Richards 403) makes all manner of basket ware. Snailtrail Weavers (0239) 74228 at Penwenallt Farm, Cilgerran (Mid Way Motors 430) have a studio showing handspun Welsh fleece rugs and other things being made. Also at Cilgerran is Jean Wilkes Ceramic Workshop, Porth-y-Castell (0239) 614258 specialising in Egyptian faience. Old

Forge Crafts (09947) 241 at Alltybont, Llanglydwen produces traditional Welsh love spoons. Hafod Hill Pottery (09946) 361 is a small country pottery making handthrown and wood-fired stoneware pots. Bryn Pottery (023979) 608 at Eglwyswrw demonstrates traditional techniques with modern decorative work.

Woodmagic (0239 74) 431 at Yet Wen near Boncath (Mid Way Motors 430) makes traditional and original wooden toys. Glyn-y-fran Woodcraft, at Pentregalar (0239) 73347 makes a range of high quality woodcraft, as does Philip Layton, woodturner (0239) 820469 at Fachongle, near Newport (Richards 412). Pembrokeshire Crafts, Newport (0239) 820851 specialises in making furniture from English oak and other hardwoods. Not far away at Cilgwyn (0239) 820470 is the Cilgwyn Candle Workshop. Kimswood Country Workshops (09912) 230 makes solid wood furniture in pine, elm and oak.

Melin Tregwynt, near Letterston (03485) 225 produces a range of classic woollens (Richards 412). Wallis Woollen Mill at Ambleston (0437) 731297 weaves a range of fabrics in pure wool using natural colours from vegetable dyes. Cemaes Pottery Workshop near Dinas Cross (03486) 376 includes a variety of handthrown domestic ware. Studio in The Church near Login (09916) 676, produces colourful handweaving in a peaceful setting. The Pottery at Wolfscastle (Richards 412) allows you to try your hand at the wheel, as does its sister workshop in St. David's. Nant-y-Coy Mill (043 787) 671 at Treffgarne has craft workshops as well as a museum. Hafod Hill Pottery at Llanboidy (09946) 361 makes hand-thrown and wood-fired pots for kitchen and table use. The Cottage Garden Pottery near Haverfordwest (0437) 610 has a wide range of pottery and porcelain, as does the Pembrokeshire Pottery (0437) 710628 at Keeston Hill. Honeyborough Pottery (0646) 600013 (South Wales Transport 359) makes a range of handmade stoneware. Stoney Park Woollen Weavers (0834) 813868 demonstrate traditional weaving of tweeds and rugs, ties and caps.

Narberth Pottery (0834) 860732 makes individually-painted pots and other items for the home, as does Begelly Pottery (0834) 811204 near Kilgetty. Avondale Glass, Kilgetty (0834) 813345 demonstrates the art of glass making and Inwood (0834) 812152 at nearby Cold Inn shows the skill of woodcarving, especially love spoons. The Saundersfoot Pottery specialises in handthrown ceramic ware. Penally Pottery (0834) 3796, near Tenby hand models stoneware characters and fantasy scenes. Tenby Pottery (0834) 2890 produces a wide range of useful decorative high-fired earthenware. The Siop Fach (03483) 379 at Mathry allows you to see the woodturners producing all manner of things from ash, oak, yew and elm. The Carvers' Workshop (0646) 636361 at Marloes produces relief and three-dimensional wildlife carvings. The Woollen Mill, Middle Hill, Solva (Richards 340) specialises in carpets and rugs.

Marchnadoedd Crefft Sir Benfro (Pembrokeshire Craft Markets) arranges craft markets all the year round throughout the county.

**Wholefoods:** Y Felin (0239) 613999, a water driven mill at St. Dogmaels, produces traditional stoneground wholemeal flour and offers tasty food in the tea room. Mother Earth Delicatessen in Fishguard and Wholefoods of Newport in Dolphin Street both sell wholefoods. Cnapan Country House, also in Newport, which offers fresh local produce and vegetarian meals is well-known locally, as is the superb Tregynon Country Farm Hotel in the nearby Gwaun Valley. The latter two also offer accommodation. Fishguard Market is interesting and the Bwyd-y-Byd sells wholefoods. Near Fishguard, at Castle Morris, Llangloffan Farm (03485) 241 allows visitors to watch their traditional cheese-making, as does Nevern Dairy near Newport.

Crymych has a wholefood shop, Bwyd-y-Byd, and not far away is the Gwelfor Country Guest House which offers homely accommodation and vegetarian wholefoods. The Natural Grocer and Wholefood Restaurant, Quay Street, Haverfordwest offers refreshment. Food For Though in Milford Haven sells wholefood. Castell Hywell Farmhouse Dairy (083 483) 201 at Lampeter Velfrey near Narberth produces fine cheeses in a home dairy. The Wholefood Heron and Ted's Wholefoods both of Main Street, Pembroke sell a range of good food as does The Granary non-smoking restaurant. The delicatessen at Charlett's the Butcher's sells a fine range of local cheeses. Maesglas at St. David's has an alternative takeaway. The Pilgrim's Restaurant in St. David's prepares unusual dishes. A veritable feast all round.

**Community initiatives:** The West Wales Energy Group acts as a forum to promote the efficient use of energy and re-usable resources. Contact (03486) 421.

Dyfed Wildlife Trust, 7 Market Street, Haverfordwest (0437) 765462 aims to safeguard Dyfed's precious natural heritage through acquisition of nature reserves, an educational programme, cooperating with landowners and government agencies in improving the countryside for wildlife and by monitoring potential dangers and protecting threatened species.

The Stepaside Heritage Project is working on the restoration of the nineteenth-century Kilgetty ironworks with an interpretive centre, guided walks, a vintage coach, etc. (0384) 811686.

The Orielton Field Centre, Pembroke, is an educational charity offering week-long courses relating to environmental studies, ecology and marine biology.

Taff Cleddau Rural Initiative aims to improve the social and economic well-being of rural communities within the Narberth and Whitland area.

Myles Pepper, West Wales Art Centre, encourages artistic activities for young people.

# Coastline and vales
# of Dyfed

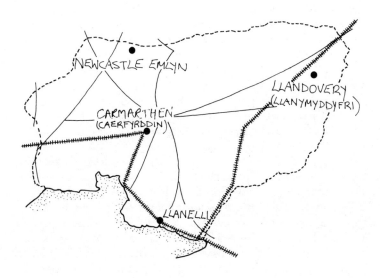

Between the Teifi and the Tywi lies a much underrated part of Wales, far too often bypassed by those rushing to the beaches of South Pembrokeshire. The area embraces the lower range of the Cambrian Mountains near Llanymyddyfri (Llandovery) and Llandeilo as well as a coastal fringe from the endless sands of Pendine to those of Pembrey near Llanelli.

As in the remainder of Dyfed, the uplands are the result of an uplift of rock strata in Silurian times and nearer to the coast the rocks are softer and less resistant to erosion. The main economic activity is still farming, although there is a small amount of coalmining in the east and a manufacturing base around Llanelli. It is an area of contrasts – from wild windswept moorlands between Lampeter and

99

the upper reaches of the Tywi at Llyn Brianne to an urbanised coastal fringe.

Woodland remnants of oak, ash and sycamore survive, particularly in the tributary valleys of the Teifi between Caerfyrddin (Carmarthen) and Llandeilo and around Llanelli, with a host of birds from pied flycatcher to woodpecker. However, major tracts of land have been put to coniferous afforestation as at Brechfa, Caeo and Rhandirmwyn as well as at Pembrey on the coast. This has been a major change of land use, with the inevitable knock-on effects on wildlife and farming.

Caerfyrddin (Carmarthen) is the largest of the market towns and has a small industrial area based on the river. The Tywi estuary is delightful as the train sweeps around the coast into Kidwelly, an old fishing community with a small tourist and boating interest. Across the waters lie the impressive Llansteffan Castle and the unpretentious village of the same name beyond, not much altered since the last century. Laugharne attracts more visitors, as it was once home to writer and poet Dylan Thomas.

To the north lies Newcastle Emlyn, a gorgeous little market town on the banks of the Teifi and by far the best place to stay to discover the river's secrets. Llandysul and Llanbydder, market towns in their own right especially known for horse fairs, deserve attention, as does the small town of Pencader. The other area to explore is around Llanymyddyfri and Llandeilo in the Tywi Valley. This has its own charms and you will find pubs where a pint of Felinfoel or Buckleys is downed between a yarn or two and shops that have resisted the changing mood of the last two decades and survived.

It is also an area where Green awareness is growing and environmental groups here and in the Llanelli area strive to raise these issues for public discussion. The wind power demonstration area at Burry Port will fascinate the Green traveller, not the prettiest of sites but an interesting tour nevertheless.

**Tourist information:** Caerfyrddin (Carmarthen) Tourist Information Office, Lammas Street (0267) 231557; Llandovery Tourist Information Office (0550) 20693; Newcastle Emlyn Tourist Information Office, Market Hall (0239) 711333.

**Transport:** The area is served by British Rail from Swansea to Llandeilo and Llanymyddyfri (Llandovery) on the Heart of Wales line, and through to Caerfyrddin (Carmarthen) and Whitland.

Llanelli is the junction for the Heart of Wales line and Caerfyrddin (Carmarthen) serves as the main interchange for buses to Newcastle Emlyn and surrounding area. The routes are shown on the Dyfed public transport map. Most places are accessible by public transport, with the exception of some of the quieter villages and hamlets in the west and north of the area. The postbuses out of Llanymyddyfri (Llandovery) to Rhandirmwyn or to Myddfai, the home of mystical physicians down the ages, are a must, as is the market day run between Llandeilo and Lampeter (Thomas Brothers service 284).

The Teifi Steam Railway (0559) 371077 at Henllan (Crosville Wales 400) near Llandysul offers good views of the Teifi Valley and the Gwili Railway (0267) 230666 at Bronwydd Arms station (Davies Bros. 460, 461) winds its way for a short section alongside the River Gwili.

Cycles can be hired from Roman Road Cycle Tours, Ddol-Las, Ffarmers (055 85) 336.

**Access to the countryside:** In the north-western part of this area, the countryside around Newcastle Emlyn and in the Teifi valley is gentle and beautiful with local walks around Newcastle Emlyn, Henllan and at Cenarth Falls. The lanes to the south of the Teifi are ideal for cycling, through hamlets such as Cwmcych and Talog and Abernant, lost to the world en route to Carmarthen.

To the east Dinefwr, with its two principal towns of Llanymyddyfri (Llandovery) and Llandeilo, is threaded by country lanes ideal for cycling to such attractions as the Dolaucothi Gold Mines at Pumsaint or Talley Abbey. Walking is good when it comes to drovers' tracks through the wild mountains to Tregaron or Lampeter, but local paths are less easy to find. Gelli Aur Country Park, two miles west of Llandeilo, offers nature trails, an arboretum and guided walks. Dinefwr Park and Castle has a number of marked walks. Also worth a visit is Carreg Cennen Castle, with stunning views from a local walk as well as a rare breeds farm. Northwest of Llanymyddyfri is Llyn Brianne Reservoir with local walks. Nearby are the Dinas bird reserve and Twm Sion Catti's Cave. Llanymyddyfri has a local riverside walk, leaflet available. There are also leaflets outlining walks in the western fringe of the Brecon Beacons National Park. The Blaencwm Wildfowl Reserve at Salem near Llandeilo is open to the public.

The Caerfyrddin (Carmarthen) Group of the Rambler's Association produces a leaflet of footpaths and walks near to the town. There are also guided town trails during the summer months. Access to the coast allows some walking near Pendine, Laugharne (South Wales Transport 222) and Llansteffan (Jones 227). There is a good walk over the hills between Ferryside on the Tywi estuary and Kidwelly (Davies Brothers 198). There are miles of walks along Pembrey Sands, now a country park offering guided walks and a host of other facilities. The Wildfowl and Wetlands Trust is establishing a centre at Penclawydd in the spring of 1991 overlooking an 150-acre salt marsh where pintail, redshank, short-eared owls and peregrines can be seen along with dozens of wildfowl.

On the outskirts of Llanelli is a country walk around the Lower Llieda Reservoir in mixed woodland with good views. There is also a good town trail leaflet reflecting local heritage.

**Museums:** The Museum of the Welsh Woollen Industry (0559) 370929 at Dre-fach (Davies 462) illustrates the history of wool-production in earlier times. At Caerfyrddin (Carmarthen) is a museum with a local section. Nearby at Cynwyl Elfed is 'Y Gangell', the former home of local poet Dr Elfet Lewis, Archdruid and Hymnologist, which is open to the public. At Laugharne the Boathouse (0994) 427420 reflects the life and times of Dylan Thomas. A museum at Kidwelly (0554) 891078 records the industrial past of the area, particularly handmade tinplate production.

The area is dotted with castles – Newcastle Emlyn, Caerfyrddin (Carmarthen), Llansteffan, Dryslwyn, Llanymyddyfri (Llandovery), Cennen Carreg and Kidwelly.

**Bookshops:** Fred Cooper Books in the Market Hall at Newcastle Emlyn has an interest in Welsh books and keeps a small stock of Green books. Imago by the bridge has a wide range of books on astrology, health and healing and meditation, and offers astrology services. The New Bookshop in Llanymyddyfri has a range of local and countryside books. Picton Books in Lammas Street, Caerfyrddin has a small selection of Green books and Siop y Pentan in the New Market has a local section.

**Craft workshops:** Just outside Newcastle Emlyn at Greenhill House, Pentrecagal (Davies 460-462) is a handmade paper workshop (0559) 370088 producing paper from plants and recycled paper. Near Llandysul is the Acres Beach Gallery (055932) 2329 at Derw Mill, Pentrecwrt. Also near Llandysul is Brambles Patchwork at Bancyfford.

Kittywake Perfumes at Taliaris, Llandeilo makes high quality perfumes from plants. The Trapp Art and Craft Centre (0269) 850362 near Llandeilo shows craftspeople at work and arranges courses and demonstrations. The Gear Wheel Gallery at Y Felin Rhydcymerau (0558) 685220 also displays work of local craftspeople and runs short courses. Nearby at Pempompren are Janet and Roger Quilter (0558) 685514 who specialise in making quilts, cushions and waistcoats. The Brianne Craft Woodworkers (05504) 315 at Bryncapel, Gwynfe near Llangadog make traditional woodware.

Near Caerfyrddin (Carmarthen), the Gwili Pottery (0267 84) 449 at Pontsarsais demonstrates handthrown pottery making.

**Wholefood:** Hives in Sycamore Street, Newcastle Emlyn sells products made at the nearby Felin Geri Mill (see Ceredigion for details) and some local organically-grown vegetables. Albion Wholefoods in Lloyd Terrace sells a range of goods. Caws Cenarth, a handmade award winning Caerfilli cheese, is produced at Fferm Glyneithiniog above the Afon Cych to the west of Penrherber crossroads. The cows graze on insecticide-free pastures and the making of the vegetarian cheese can be seen at the farm. It is off the beaten track and well worth a visit, but check opening times (0239) 710432 before travelling. Just a little to the south Mountpleasant Goat Farm near Trelech offers cheese-making demonstrations.

Iechyd Da, Broad Street, Llanymyddyfri sells a good range of organic produce and other items. Apps (0558) 823099, Ty Isaf, Trapp near Llandeilo has a restaurant offering vegetarian dishes. Felin Newydd (05585) 375, a 200-year old mill at Crugybar, produces stoneground wholemeal flour in a traditional manner and sells locally-made cheeses as well as other goods.

Aardvark Wholefoods, Mansell Street in Carmarthen sells wholefoods, as does the Waverley Stores in Lammas Street which also has a vegetarian restaurant. Yr Hen Dafarn at Llansteffan is a former inn now serving fine vegetarian dishes in a cafe and restaurant.

**Health:** *The Herbal Remedies of the Physicians of Myddfai* provides a fascinating insight into herbal medicines of previous eras.

**Energy:** The Carmarthen Bay Wind Energy Demonstration Centre (05546) 4989 at Burry Port (train or bus from Llanelli) allows the visitor to see at first hand the capability of several wind turbines on a stretch of coast by a disused coal-fired station. Different pieces of equipment are being tested here for use in the UK and overseas.

**Co-operatives:** Trosol Cyf (0239) 710717 offers language translation. Cymdeithas Yr Hen Gapel, Pencader is a village community initiative.

**Community initiatives:** Teifi Valley Friends of the Earth meet regularly at The Granary, Aberteifi. Contact (0239) 615066.

Glanhelyg at Llechryd offers courses in painting, tai chi, yoga, circle dancing, etc. Contact Robert and Rachel Holtom on (0239) 87482.

Bro Brianne Community Arts council stimulates local interest in the arts. Contact Mrs. Sheila Jones, Pantllech Farm, Rhandirmyn (05506) 261.

The Green Group runs a stall in Llandeilo market every Friday, proceeds going to environmental concerns. Contact Friends of the Earth on (0558) 685353.

Green farming courses are arranged at Caerfyrddin (Carmarthen) College of Technology.

# *Brecon and the Beacons*

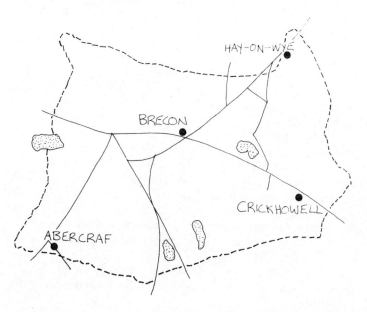

Unlike many of the other upland areas of Wales, the Brecon Beacons consist of a large tract of old red sandstone, which gives way to carboniferous limestone and millstone grits where it meets that major rift of the Neath Valley. The twin summits of Corn Du and Pen-y-Fan (886 metres) are landmarks for miles around and it is from these peaks that the Brecon Beacons take their name. In many ways it is easiest to visualise the Beacons as four distinct groups of high ground, the Black Mountain in the west between Llandeilo and Brynamman, Fforest Fawr north of the Heads of the Valleys road, a central block between Merthyr, Brecon and Crickhowell and lastly the Black Mountains between Hay-on-Wye and Abergavenny. Outside the National Park, to the west of Brecon and north of Sennybridge, along the ridges of Mynydd Epynt, is a fifth mountain area, but this is heavily dominated by the military for training and thus unfortunately is very much out of bounds.

It is these high level glacier-sculptured uplands which form much of the Brecon Beacons National Park although it extends to the broad valley of the river Usk. Farming is tough and farmsteads are isolated except in the more sheltered valleys. Talybont Lake is considered to be important for wildlife as is Llangorse Lake, although the latter can get very crowded with visitors at times.

The Black Mountains are perhaps the most impressive section of border country, with brooding masses standing over the gentle county of Herefordshire. This area is beloved by pony-trekkers and walkers following Offa's Dyke Path to Capel-y-ffin and Llanthony.

As one would expect, these isolated uplands were inhabited by prehistoric tribes, with remains of cairns, enclosures and stone circles found on higher slopes. The settlements of recent centuries are invariably at crossings of rivers. Brecon is the largest and in fact is overlooked by an Iron Age hill fort at Pen-y-Crug. It is a lively town with a good market place around the Bulwark. Amazingly, it was linked to the industrialised world by the Monmouthshire and Brecon Canal and in recent years this delightful rural cut has been restored for leisure use.

Crickhowell is steeped in history and its castle and nearby Tretower Court are reminders of its strategic defensive position in the Usk Valley.

Hay-on-Wye is not what one would expect. During the past two decades it has become a world centre for secondhand books and through this fame has come to this once sleepy Welsh market town on the banks of the Wye. The fabric of the town has changed little but the atmosphere has, in some ways for the better and in others for the worse. Travel there on a Thursday when the market day buses bring people in from the outlying villages and the stalls are laid out in the streets.

Near Hay is the village of Clyro, where Francis Kilvert wrote his now famous diaries. The locality is often referred to as Kilvert Country, which is probably making him turn in his grave for he loathed the idea of tourists! Not far away are Bronllys and Talgarth, Llangors and Llangynidr and to the west of Brecon Trecastle and

Sennybridge. These villages, along with smaller hamlets such as Velindre, Cwmdu, and Lower and Upper Chapel welcome the visitor looking for a quieter place to stay.

**Tourist information:** Brecon Tourist Information Centre, Cattle Market (0874) 2485; Hay-on-Wye Tourist Information Office, Craft Centre, Oxford Road (0497) 820144.

**Transport:** Brecon lost its railway network more than two decades ago and in many respects the main bus network reflects the replacement efforts of the 1960s. The main access to Brecon is a daily bus service (Silverline) from Merthyr Tydfil rail station (including Sundays). Another important bus route is by way of Abergavenny (mainly National Welsh, but Silverline run one bus on a Sunday from the railway station), where the bus station is five minutes walk from the railway station. There is a good route from Hereford to Hay-on-Wye and Brecon (National Welsh) and a slightly less frequent service between Brecon and Swansea (Silverline). The service to Llandrindod Wells (Roy Brown) is infrequent. Unfortunately, access to the Black Mountains by bus is non-existent.

The Beacons Rambler is a service provided by Silverline buses between Merthyr and Brecon every day during the summer including a special service on Sundays. There are special return tickets available as well as a booklet full of self-guided walks from the Rambler that is useful for both the casual walker and the serious rambler.

The Brecon Mountain Railway (0685) 4854 operates from the outskirts of Merthyr (National Welsh) to offer access to walks around Pontsticill Reservoir.

**Access to the countryside:** The Brecon Beacons National Park provides tremendous scope for walking for those who enjoy mountain climbs and high ranges. Dozens of publications, many from the National Park itself, give information on walks. There is a programme of guided walks and discovery days to suit most abilities, including superb minibus tours to isolated parts of the park on certain days. They operate from the Brecon Beacons Mountain Centre (0874) 3366, which is a mile off the A470 from Libanus School (Silverline). Similar walks and adventure days are organised by Craig-y-nos Country Park north of Ystradgynlais (Silverline). Dan-Yr-Ogof showcaves are nearby. There are also shorter and easier walks in and around the towns of Brecon, Crickhowell, and

Hay-on-Wye. Offa's Dyke passes through the latter and continues over the Black Mountains.

There are a few open farms such as Waun Newydd (087482) 8133 at Crai, near Sennybridge (nearest bus, Silverline) which welcome family groups or small parties of visitors, but phone to check first.

The Monmouthshire and Brecon Canal offers gentle towpath walking. Those who enjoy boats can hire them from Cambrian Boats (087486) 315 at Ty Newydd, Pencelli (National Welsh) on a half-day or day basis as well as for longer periods. Cycle hire is also available from here. Rowing boats may be hired for an outing on Llangorse Lake at Lakeside Boat Hire (0874 84) 226.

Dragon-Fly Canal Boat Trips (087 486) 382 offer tours from the Brecon basin along the Monmouthshire and Brecon Canal.

**Museums:** The Brecknock Museum in Brecon holds a local collection.

**Bookshops:** Gwyn Evans in The Struet, Brecon, has a selection of local books. Hay-on-Wye is the largest centre for secondhand/ antiquarian books in the world and the town is swamped with bookshops specialising in everything from bees to utopian societies.

**Craft workshops:** A variety of craftspeople can be seen at the Hay-on-Wye Craft Workshop. The Glynderi Pottery (087482) 564 at Sennybridge (Silverline) makes stoneware pottery and potters can also be seen at work at The Pottery (0874) 754388, Llyswen. The Black Mountain Pottery at Llanelieu Court (0874) 711518 near Talgarth offers pottery and painting.

**Wholefood:** Top Drawer shops in Brecon specialise in Welsh farmhouse cheeses and other good foods. The Granary Restaurant in Hay-on-Wye is well-known for its wholefood. Wholesnax in Trecastle makes wholefood snacks.

**Health:** The Country Herb Garden near Brynamman, a co-operative, manufactures herb-based products and remedies (0639) 842808.

**Community initiatives:** The Brecknock Wildlife Trust can be contacted at Lion Yard, Brecon. Brecon Friends of the Earth specialises in recycling products. Details can be found in local libraries.

The Guildhall, Brecon encourages the staging of local productions and the Brycheiniog Association for the Arts publishes a *What's On* bulletin.

# Swansea, Mumbles and Gower

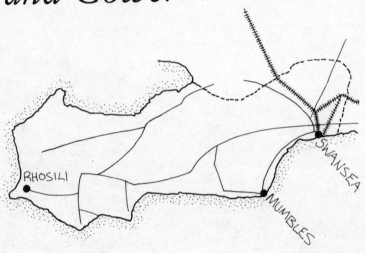

The Gower peninsula, its beautifully-sandy beaches sandwiched between limestone cliffs, and with sandstone moorland ridges and commons, is much loved by the people of Glamorgan. It also has large saltmarshes such as Llanrhidan and Landimore facing the Loughor Estuary. Not far away is Penclawdd, where oyster catchers comb the sands for cockles in competition with some of the last remaining cocklers in Wales. Laverbread, traditionally made from seaweed, is still enjoyed by local people, although it is very much a speciality.

The coastal resorts of Mumbles, Caswell, Oxwich and Rhosili are extremely busy on hot summer Sundays, with lengthy traffic queues making the whole exercise seem pointless. It is, however, surprising

110

that it is not worse, given the close proximity to such a large urban area, and the resorts are refreshingly quiet mid-week and out of season. Leave the beaches and take to the paths around Port Eynon, at one time an oyster fishing port, or between the villages of Llangenydd or Llanmadoc or down to Rhosili to see the ancient chambers and mounds. Travel to Reynoldston, which is a good base for short walks to Arthur's Stone or the other stones and Celtic crosses in this area, perched on the central sandstone spine. These are the quieter haunts.

Swansea is a jumble of a place with shopping, industry and maritime influence. The South Dock development is interesting, even though it has its critics. Swansea has a Green movement seeking to highlight conservation, energy and peace issues. The Swansea Cycle Path allows access out into the countryside and a further extension into the Gower peninsula would be excellent.

**Tourist information:** Swansea Tourist Information Centre, Singleton Street (0792) 468321.

**Transport:** Swansea is well-served by British Rail from Cardiff, West Wales and also the Heart of Wales line. There is also a large bus station with regular services to most parts including Mumbles and the Gower, although routes become fewer as they penetrate the peninsula. Throughout the summer there is a guided coach tour of Swansea city on certain days; for further information contact South Wales Transport (SWT) on (0792) 475511.

There is cycle hire at Clyne Valley Cycles (0792) 208889 which is by the Swansea Cycle Path at Dunvant (SWT 21).

**Access to the countryside:** There are miles of good walks along the Gower coast and West Glamorgan County Council produces a selection of walks leaflets and booklets to assist the rambler. A large country park in the Clyne valley (SWT 1, 2, 3) has walks, trails and cycleways. The National Trust Visitor Centre at Rhosili (SWT 18) is a good place to pick up ideas for local walks, as is the National Nature Reserve and Centre at Oxwich where there are guided tours. Whiteford Burrows Nature Reserve is also superb for walking and wildlife.

**Museums:** The Maritime and Industrial Museum in Swansea is only a walk from Swansea city centre. The Swansea Museum in Victoria Road is the oldest museum in Wales, with a traditional mix

111

of displays. The Gower Farm Museum (065671) 2572 at Llandewi near Reynoldston (SWT 18b) has reconstructed farm life at the beginning of the twentieth century, and also offers good farm trails of between 2 and 6 miles.

**Bookshops:** Dillons and Peters bookshops in Swansea have local and environmental sections.

**Craft workshops:** The Glynn Vivian Art Gallery in central Swansea is recognised as a community centre for the development of local arts.

**Wholefoods:** Ear to the Ground, a local co-operative based at Bryn-y-Mor Road, Swansea, offers a range of products, as does Roots Wholefood and Vegetarian Restaurant at Mumbles. Chris's Kitchen at Swansea market is a popular stop for the Green traveller and sells laverbread too.

**Health:** Dr. J. Sewell, Pinewood Road, Uplands, Swansea is a member of the British Holistic Medical Association.

**Co-operatives:** A number of co-operatives exist in the Swansea area, including Abba Cabs (0792) 702333 if you are in need of a taxi in Swansea and A&M Taxis at Pontardawe (0792) 830241 to the north of the city. At the Fish Market Swansea Fishermen Ltd. runs a co-op and Roots (Swansea) Ltd. (0792) 366006 offers vegetarian wholefoods.

**Community initiatives:** The Gower Society is involved in conservation issues. Contact (0792) 368439.

# Cardiff and the South Wales Coast

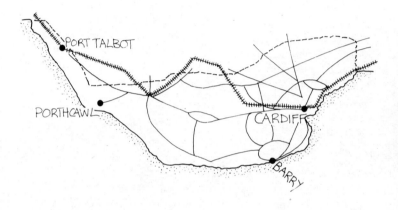

The South Wales coast from the Afon Neath to Cardiff Bay is predominantly coastal plain with ribbon housing and industrial development interspersed with lowland farming in the Vale of Glamorgan. There are long beaches at Aberavon, Kenfig and Porthcawl, as well as smaller inlets south of Ogmore-by-Sea. Dunes and saltmarshes add to the variety of wildlife along the coast, which has been designated a Heritage Coast and needs every bit of help it can get to avoid gross pollution from nearby towns and cities. Kenfig Pool, between Margam and Porthcawl, is a freshwater site attracting hundreds of waterfowl including pochard and bewick swans.

Off the coast near Penarth lies Flat Holm, a windswept island of rough ground populated mainly by seagulls. It is thought to be one of the few locations where the wild Welsh leek still flourishes. Access to the island is restricted.

The major road and rail arteries cutting across the Vale of Glamorgan have virtually become a dividing line, with a more rural farming base close to the sea and industrial or dormitory development around and to the north of the routes. Between Bridgend and Barry are several surprisingly interesting towns, such as Cowbridge and Llantwit Major, with narrow streets on a medieval grid and an architectural mix which is pleasing to the eye. Further along the coast are the ports of Barry and Penarth, the latter being home to the famous paddle steamer Waverley.

Cardiff is what one would expect of a capital. It is bustling, has an air of confidence and is packed with places to visit. It is the centre of Welsh broadcasting and other Welsh institutions such as Cardiff Arms Park national stadium and the National Museum. The River Taff and surrounding parks bring air to the city and there are lovely walks up along the Taff Valley to Llandaff Cathedral and Castle Coch.

The docks are being re-developed in Cardiff, as are some of the shopping areas. Let us hope the blend of modern and old, arcade alongside shopping precinct, re-used warehouse aside new office block, works. There are other projects which should make Cardiff a better place to live in and visit. The City Farm in Sloper Road is a venture which could well be duplicated elsewhere and The Peace Shop in Roath endeavours to bring to the fore peace and environmental issues. The idea of re-introducing more woodland into the area, Coedwig Caerdydd, is a good one, as are the plans to improve the cycleway network into the Valleys and to the old docks. These should not be marginal projects but mainstream initiatives considered as important as any strategic road link.

Cardiff offers the visitor a more relaxed stay than many capitals, is full of interest and it is where you change for the Valleys or the Vale of Glamorgan. Stop off on your travels.

**Tourist information:** Barry Tourist Information Centre, The Promenade (0446) 747171; Cardiff Tourist Information Centre, 8-14 Bridge Street (0222) 227281; Porthcawl Tourist Information Office, The Old Police Station, John Street (0656) 716639; Port Talbot Bagle Brook Tourist Information Centre, Beefeater Restaurant, Sunnycroft Road, Baglan (0639) 823049; Sarn Tourist Information Centre, Junction 36, near Bridgend (0656) 654906.

**Transport:** Cardiff is very well served by trains. There is also a regular service to the key towns along the coastal strip to Swansea, Bridgend, Port Talbot and Neath. Penarth and Barry are served by the Valley Lines rail network. Other towns and villages are provided with good bus routes, usually hourly or more often, including journeys into the South Wales Valleys. The major company is National Welsh, so phone (0222) 371331 for up-to-the-minute information, but there are others such as Jones Motors of Pontypridd, Silverline of Merthyr Tydfil and Cynon Valley Transport of Aberdare. The main company in Cardiff is Cardiff Bus (0222) 396521; they offer a 'Capital' day rover ticket, as do National Welsh in conjunction with Red and White, so between them they cover most of eastern South Wales.

Two tours can be taken in Cardiff, 'The Cardiff Experience' provided by Croeso Tours (0222) 395173 and an open-top bus ride that Cardiff Bus (0222) 396521 has introduced with a number of variations on the same theme.

Those who enjoy seafaring will head straight for Penarth Pier (direct bus link from Cardiff) to join the paddle steamer Waverley or cruise ship Balmoral (0446) 720656.

Even in Cardiff, cycle hire is not easily available, which perhaps says something about the traffic. Try Mike Thanes' Garage, Caerffilli Road (0222) 623854. There is however the Three Castles cycle route, which links Cardiff Castle and Castle Coch (see below) and there will hopefully be extensions south to the docks. In fact, if proposals go ahead for using disused railway lines as on part of the Penarth to Sully cycle way, there should be a considerable improvement. The exciting Taff Trail walkway and cycle route between Cardiff and Brecon should also be a boon to the Green traveller when it comes to fruition.

**Access to the countryside:** Even though this is the most densely populated part of Wales, there are still dozens of opportunities to walk in quieter areas away from main roads. The coastline from Aberavon to Barry offers a number of splendid short walks and the Glamorgan Heritage Coast project aims to improve access throughout and has published a number of leaflets. Porthcawl produces a pleasant town trail self-guided leaflet.

Margam Park near Port Talbot offers 800 acres of parkland for walking and other outdoor activities. Bryngarw Country Park north of Bridgend (Bus 172) offers a variety of landscapes and habitats for

115

the discerning walker. The Kenfig Pool Nature Reserve, west of Porthcawl (National Welsh K1, 2, 3) is a freshwater lake in sand dunes with a healthy wildfowl population.

At Hensol Forest near Welsh St. Donats are a number of way-marked trails. Dyffryn Gardens (0222) 593328 is one of the finest Edwardian gardens in Wales with plenty of landscaped walks (National Welsh X2 to St. Nicholas and a short walk). Porthkerry Country Park, between Barry and Rhoose, has 220 acres of woodland with nature trails and walks. Comeston Lakes Country Park includes an area set aside for conservation of wildlife.

From Cardiff a superb walk up the Taff valley leads to Castle Coch, a Gothic fantasy castle standing on beautifully-wooded slopes. This walk is part of the Taff Valley Heritage Trail and is outlined in *Great Walks from Welsh Railways*.

**Museums:** An intriguing museum, if it can be called that, is Cosmeston medieval village (0222) 708686 near Penarth (National Welsh P4, 5, 8) where medieval dwellings are being authentically reconstructed on their original foundations after archaeological exploration.

The Cowbridge Museum Trust, High Street, Cowbridge offers a local collection.

The National Museum of Wales in Cardiff really is the treasure house of the nation, unfolding the story of Wales from earliest times.

Another section of it is the Welsh Folk Museum in St Fagans, which should be on your checklist as it is packed with open air displays of Welsh tradition and culture (Cardiff Bus 32). As part of the docks restoration there are two new attractions, Techniquest – which is a 'hands on' science centre – and the Industrial and Maritime Museum. They are near Bute Road station; or catch Cardiff Bus 6 or 7. Cardiff Castle is also worth a visit.

**Bookshops:** R. & J. McConville in Station Road, Port Talbot are a newsagent which stocks books by local authors. The Bookshop, Lias Road, Porthcawl has a section on the environment and local books. Springs in Church Street, Llantwit Major and Greeners in Broad Street, Barry have local and environmental sections.

In Cardiff, most bookshops stock fairly large sections on the environment and local books. Dillons in St. David's Shopping Centre has a good Welsh section.

**Craft workshops:** The Old Wool Barn Craft Centre at Cowbridge was formerly the collecting place for fleeces but is now a working craft centre. Nearby are the Ewenny Pottery (0656) 653020 and Claypits Pottery, both at Ewenny near Bridgend (National Welsh V3). The Model House in Llantrisant (National Welsh 241, 244, G4) is based in an old workhouse which is now the home of several craftspeople (0443) 237758.

In Cardiff the Craft Centre in The Old Library, The Hayes, displays the work of the Makers Guild in Wales, emphasising high quality craftwork.

**Wholefood:** See Green Wholefood Coffee Bar at 3 James Street, Porthcawl also sells other environmentally-sound goods. In Llantwit Major, Country Foods in East View Street sells some wholefoods, as do Health and Herbs and Diamond's Delicatessen, both in Holton Road, Barry. Healthy Foods on Ely Valley Road in Barry sells some wholefoods.

Cardiff has several wholefood shops and cafes, including: Crumbs, Morgan Arcade; Wallys, Royal Arcade; New York Deli, High Street Arcade; Bean Freaks, St. Marys Street; Pulse, Kings Road, Canton; Cardiff Wholefood, Fitzroy Street, Cathays; Munchies, Crwys Road; and Sage, Wellfield Court, Roath.

**Health:** There is a South Glamorgan Homeopathic Group, details from (0222) 613266.

**Co-operatives:** Cardiff has a smattering of unusual co-operatives, such as Actors Management Wales Ltd (0222) 489032 which offers a personal management service in Wales with a bilingual policy. The WOT Theatre Group (0222) 223752 is an artists' co-operative. Riverside Architectural Ltd. (0222) 371041 is a community architects' practice. Trosol Cyf (0222) 342216 offers translation services. Honno (0222) 515014 publishes books by women in Welsh and English, with some superb material to date. If in need of a taxi in Cardiff call Amber Cars Taxi Co-operative Ltd. (0222) 378378.

**Community initiatives:** The Port Talbot Angling Club has been involved in a project to clean up the River Afan where salmon are returning after years of absence. Port Talbot Borough Council has a public campaign to make Port Talbot the cleanest town in the UK.

Glamorgan Wildlife Trust can be contacted at The Nature Centre, Tondu, Bridgend (0656) 724100.

Friends of the Earth, Wales is based at 3 James Street, Porthcawl (0656) 715185, as is See Green, a shop devoted to selling environmentally-friendly products.

The Ogwr Community Environmental Improvement Scheme has produced a number of leaflets illustrating countryside access around Bridgend, Wick, St. Brides and Ewenny. The leaflets also indicate recycling opportunities and are available locally.

The Glamorgan Trust for Nature is at Fountain, Tondu, Bridgend. Ogwr Groundwork Trust at Bryngarw near Bridgend is concerned with environmental improvement projects.

Theatr Berwyn, Natymoel, Ogmore Vale is keen to encourage community theatre initiatives.

Seawatch Centre, Summerhouse Point near Llantwit Major, is concerned with Glamorgan's coastline.

Barry and Penarth Town Councils have produced interesting local guides. Flat Holm Project, Old Police Station, Harbour Road, Barry (0446) 747661 aims to encourage conservation on the island.

Glamorgan Heritage Coast Project, The Heritage Centre, Seamouth, Southerndown, Bridgend (0656) 880157 is concerned with the conservation of this fascinating stretch of coastline.

The Cardiff there are several interesting community initiatives. The Peace Shop, Mackintosh Place, Roath (Cardiff Bus 82) is not only a shop and café, but also a resource centre run on a co-operative basis for local groups engaged in the peace movement. The Chapter Arts Centre, Market Road, Canton is one of Europe's largest and most dedicated centres for contemporary art (Cardiff Bus 12, 14, 17, 19).

*Radio Active Times*, RAT for short, is a lively magazine with a round-up of peace initiatives in South and West Wales. CND Cymru can be contacted on (0766) 831356 and Women For Peace on (0222) 226049.

Fferm Dinas Caerdydd (The City Farm), Sloper Road, Grangetown is a registered charity which aims to introduce farm life to the community and also to provide work skills.

Moves are being made to establish an environmental and resource centre for the city. Details from Glandŵr, St. Mellons Road, Lisvane, Cardiff (0222) 751736.

The Forest of Cardiff (Coedwig Caerdydd) Project (0222) 626660 aims to plant as many native broadleaf trees as possible with community support.

The Cardiff members group of the RSPB has a full programme. Details are usually available in local libraries.

Cardiff Organic Gardeners meet to discuss gardening projects. Contact (0222) 499208.

The Cardiff and South-east Wales branch of Pont, an organisation keen to improve our understanding of Wales, arranges a series of courses on the history, culture and language of Wales. Details are available at Cardiff Central Library. The Welsh Language Teaching Centre (0222) 390980 organises appropriate courses.

Cardiff City Council has devised a comprehensive recycling policy, encouraging the community to participate.

# The Vale of Usk
# and the Wye Valley

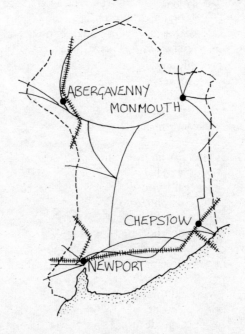

Between the Black Mountains beyond Abergavenny and the Bristol Channel lies the gently undulating land of Gwent, rich farming land full of quiet villages and historic reminders that this is the Marches, where conflict over control was the dominant local issue for centuries. It is broken up by tributaries of the Usk and pockets of mixed woodland. To the west is an industrial belt from Newport to Pontypool and to the east is the deeply incised Wye Valley, favourite of poet and painter alike.

The geology of the area is predominantly old red sandstone, with limestone ridges and cappings of millstone grit such as Sugar Loaf summit above Abergavenny and the haunting Ysgyryd Fawr, the

Skirrid. The coastal area to the south is known as the Monmouthshire Moors, rough land grazed by cattle running down to the sea defences and mud and silt flats of the Bristol Channel, and frequented by waders.

The river valleys hold the greatest interest. The Usk and Wye are little polluted and attract both salmon and trout, dippers and kingfishers. The wooded Wye Valley is a dream for the naturalist with a rich variety of plants, insects, butterflies and birds found along the local paths.

The town of Newport has a maritime tradition and the famous transporter bridge is a landmark for miles around. Nearby Caerleon is one of the major Roman remains in Wales. Caerleon and Pontypool allow access to western edges and reserves such as Llandegfedd Reservoir a few miles away. Most people, however, travel on to the small towns of Usk, Raglan or Monmouth, old-fashioned places with coaching inns and small shops and squares.

Abergavenny is the eastern gateway to the Brecon Beacons. It is a busy little town that has improved in recent decades. It also allows access to the villages and hamlets on the Welsh border around the beautiful Monnow valley, to Grosmont and Skenfrith with their ruined castles and garrison churches.

The other main area of interest is the beautiful stretch of river valley between Monmouth and Chepstow. Here is the enchanting Tintern Abbey, inspiration to Wordsworth and others, which understandably attracts large numbers of visitors at times. Chepstow, a walled town of considerable character, was once a thriving port, although it is little used these days.

The treasures of Gwent are not immediately apparent when skimming through a guide book, but travel beyond the main through-routes and another world is exposed, one with which the Green traveller will have immediate affinity.

**Tourist information:** Abergavenny Tourist Information Centre, Swan Meadow (0873) 77588; Chepstow Tourist Information Centre (02912) 3772; Monmouth Tourist Information Centre, Shire Hall (0600) 3899; Newport Tourist Information Centre, Museum and Art Gallery, John Frost Square (0633) 842962; Tintern Tourist Information Centre (0291) 689431.

**Transport:** British Rail provides a good service to Newport and the Marches line serves Cwmbran, Pontypool and Abergavenny.

There is also a reasonable service between Newport and Chepstow. Bus links are good in some places but variable elsewhere, especially on Sundays. A splendid route runs between Chepstow, Tintern and Monmouth, as well as via Trelleck. Monmouth, Usk and Raglan are served from Newport and there is a less frequent route from Abergavenny to Raglan. Most services are provided by Red and White (0291) 622947 or National Welsh (0222) 371331. A number of local rural routes run out of Abergavenny, as does a postbus to Skenfrith. There is also a local postbus from Usk to Star Hill.

For canal lovers there are boats for hire at Red Line Boats, Llanover (0873) 880516, Castle Narrowboats (0873) 830001 and Roadhouse Holiday Hire Narrowboats (0873) 830240 – the latter both at Gilwern. Those looking for a canoe on the Wye should contact Monmouth Canoe Hire on (0600) 3461. Gwent has miles of rural lanes ideal for cycling. There are few cycle hire centres, one being Pedal Away just over the border in Llangarron, Herefordshire.

**Access to the countryside:** Walking in Gwent is superb, with an increasing network of footpaths open to the public. The Offa's Dyke Path and Wye Valley Walk pass through the eastern fringe of Wales, as do the Usk Valley walks. Every year Gwent County Council put together a guided walks programme for the Wye Valley and the rest of the county with details in two local leaflets. Wye Valley events tend to include cycle rides, discussions about organic farming, historic walks, etc. There are other local walks such as the Gilwern Walk (National Welsh X4), quite a few from Monmouth to places such as the Kymin and Wonastow, and also from Tintern old railway station and from the villages of Magor and Undy. The Chepstow Society has produced a lovely town trail guide available locally.

The Forestry Commission welcome walkers in the Wentwood and Tintern forests where several waymarked walks have been devised for the visitor.

Walking Holidays (independent or self-guided) are provided by Wysk Walks at Church Farm, Mitchell Troy (0600) 2176.

**Museums:** Abergavenny Castle and Museum trace the history of the town from early times and include a farmhouse kitchen and a saddler's shop display. The Hill Court Gallery, just north of the town, has a special interest in painting as a response to Welsh life and landscape.

122

The Gwent Rural Life Museum is a private collection run by the Rural Crafts Preservation Society at The Malt Barn, Usk (02913) 3777. Monmouth Museum is both a celebration of Lord Nelson and a local collection. The Model Farm Folk Museum and Countryside Centre (02915) 231 near Llangwm offers a collection of Victorian memorabilia and is set in splendid scenery. Chepstow Museum has a fascinating display about the important role of the river as a wine port and a centre for shipbuilding and salmon fishing. Caldicot Castle and Country Park (Red and White X70, Newport 64) houses a small local collection and there are currently excavations to uncover Bronze Age Caldicot. The Newport Museum and Art Gallery, John Frost Square contains a local section. The Fourteen Locks Canal Centre tells the story of the Monmouthshire canals (National Welsh 56, R1, 2, 3). The Roman amphitheatre at Caerleon is well preserved. Penhow Castle, near Newport, offers self-guided tours around the oldest lived-in castle in Wales.

The area has many other castles, such as Grosmont, Skenfirth and White Castle to the north-east of Abergavenny, Monmouth and Chepstow on the Wye, and Raglan and Usk in the Vale. Tintern Abbey has an exhibition of medieval life in one of the finest romantic settings in Wales.

**Bookshops:** In Abergavenny, The Map Shop, Monk Street, is ideal for local maps and books. Wise Owls, Frogmore Street has a small local section. In Monmouth by far the best range of Green books is at Small Planet, Agincourt Square. Chepstow Bookshop, St. Mary Street has a range of local books. Bookworm in Skinner Street, Newport has a local section.

**Craft workshops:** The Pandy Craft Shop, Ty Newydd Farm makes soft toys based on local characters (National Welsh). Wool Wheels Weaving (060084) 607, near Skenfrith and north of Monmouth, demonstrates weaving and has displays about spinning and weaving. Kirstie Buckland, 'Capper to the Quality' (0600) 2469 sells a most unusual range of traditional caps from the Monmouth Cap of the sixteenth and seventeenth centuries to the Scots Bonnet.

Brockweir Glass and the Malthouse Pottery, both at Brockweir, demonstrate craft skills. The Workshop Gallery at Chepstow illustrates the work of sculptor and potter.

There are craft workshops at Tredegar House, near Newport as well as trails and historic displays in the house (National Welsh 3, 15 and 30).

**Wholefood:** Cornucopia, Market Street, Abergavenny sells herbal remedies and health foods. In Monmouth, Small Planet, Agincourt Square, offers a wide range of foods, as does Irma Fingal, including home made bread and a good selection of cheeses.

Wye Valley Herbs at Tintern has a farm shop selling organic produce. Harvesters Health and Wholefoods on Caerleon Road has a comprehensive stock.

Newport has three shops which include restaurants – The Happy Carrot in Dock Street, Hunky Dory in Charles Street, and Lifecycle in John Frost Square.

**Health:** The West Usk Lighthouse, Lighthouse Road, Wentlooge near Newport (0633) 810126 offers healthy living breaks and has a float room for mental and physical relaxation.

**Co-operatives:** Able Taxis Newport Ltd. (0633) 59530 is a co-operative venture.

**Community initiatives:** The Hill Residential College, Abergavenny offers a wide range of creative and cultural courses (0873) 5221 including such topics as herbal remedies, health and happiness through natural therapy, the Welsh countryside, etc.

Gwent Wildlife Trust is based at 16 White Swan Court, Monmouth (0600) 5501. Wildlife in Newport Group (WING), the first urban wildlife group in Wales, can be contacted at 14 Summerhill Avenue, Newport. Its aim is to drive Newport wild and it is not doing a bad job so far.

The Friends of Monnow Bridge aim to pedestrianise the route over this unique Welsh bridge. Contact: Chippenham Gate, Monmouth, Gwent.

Greenpeace (Gwent and Glamorgan) can be contacted on (0792) 406461.

Not a community initiative as such, but an interesting venture, is the Caer Llan Field Study Centre near Monmouth (0600) 860359, where seven of the bedrooms are in the unique earth-sheltered, solar-heated Berm House, thought to be the house using the lowest amount of energy in Wales.

# The South Wales Valleys

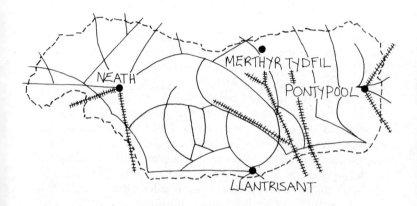

NEATH

MERTHYR TYDFIL

PONTYPOOL

LLANTRISANT

While many view the Valleys as being wholly industrial, it is fair to say that there have always been vast tracts of countryside available for recreation. For above the valleys are long open ridges, threaded with paths through moorland grasses and pockets of broad-leaved woodlands. In the valley bottoms, the distinct linear development of the last century remains where road, rail and river are squeezed together and rows of terraced houses creep up the hillsides. In many places work is in hand to bring the countryside closer to town with the development of riverside paths, tracks and country parks, and a gradual removal of the dereliction left by an earlier economy. The shift in emphasis is quite dramatic in places.

The great Neath Rift Valley is the divider between the mountain tops of the Beacons and the steep-sided valleys running south-east towards the sea. The break between rock structures, the alternation of hard gritstones and softer shales, has led to a number of spectacular waterfalls in the Henrhyd and Ystradfellte areas. The carboniferous limestone ridges overlying coal measures are softer than one would expect and drop sharply to the coastal plains. Increasingly they have been planted with fast-growing conifers.

Space does not permit more than the briefest mention of Valley communities, of the way of life that was once prevalent, of singing and chapel, of poverty and pits, of rugby and club. The industrial legacy remains, but these communities are in transition, values changing as the economic base has done. Many a writer has argued, however, that the spirit remains, a spirit of comradeship that will be in the Valleys forever.

Travel in any of the Valleys and you will find paths onto the hills. Merthyr and Blaenafon have been at pains to reflect their industrial heritage and there are several local attractions and village history trails. Ebbw Vale looms large as the last of the Garden Festivals and will take the valley through the 1990s with a renewed focus. Most people will also want to visit the Rhondda, to verify that the pictures in older geography textbooks are no longer real. The transformation has been quite marked, although the traditional view of earlier decades – minus the belching smoke – is being recreated at The Rhondda Heritage Centre.

To the south the Valleys draining into the Vale of Glamorgan are equally fascinating and in many respects the prettiest. The Afan Valley is the best for exploration by bicycle or walking but the others enable the traveller to join one of the ridgeway paths spanning the Valleys.

Without doubt, the Greening of the Valleys has begun, but there is a long way to go. This should not put you off visiting one of the most interesting parts of Wales, an experience as valuable as walking through the softer hues of the Wye or along the coast of Pembrokeshire.

**Tourist information:** Aberdulais Tourist Information Centre, Aberdulais Basin (0639) 633531; Caerphilly Tourist Information Centre, The Old Police Station, Park Lane (0222) 851378; Cwmcarn Forest Drive Visitor Centre (0495) 272001; Merthyr Tydfil Tourist Information Centre, Glebelands Street (0685) 79884; Pontypridd

Tourist Information Centre, Pontypridd Historical and Cultural Centre, The Old Bridge (0443) 402077; Pontneddfechan Tourist Information Centre, near Glynneath (0639) 721795; Tredegar Tourist Information Centre, Bryn Bach Country Park (0495) 711816.

**Transport:** British Rail runs services to Neath which is the main interchange point for the Neath Valley, and in conjunction with Mid and South Glamorgan County Councils has revitalised services into the Valleys so that there is now a regular service to Treherbert, Aberdare, Merthyr Tydfil and Rhymney. Bus links start from the railheads into the Valleys where trains no longer run. Levels of frequency are generally good. National Welsh (0222) 371331 is the major operator, but there are other companies such as Shamrock in and around Pontypridd or Silverline elsewhere. Cwmbran and Pontypool have railway stations served by trains on the Marches line, allowing access to some of the eastern Valleys.

There are proposals for cycleways using disused railways in the Valleys, and as there are plenty of those it really could be a cyclists' paradise. At present few exist. In the Afan Valley, north of Port Talbot, there is a cycle hire centre at Afan Argoed (0639) 850564. At Cwm Darren the disused railway to Bargoed is used for cycling, but as yet there is no cycle hire here. Cycles are available, however, at the Dare Valley Country Park near Aberdare.

**Access to the countryside:** In recent decades there has been a vast improvement in opening up the countryside in and around the area, very often improving derelict land left from the mining era. There are four longer paths offering spectacular walks above the Valleys: the Coed Morgannwg Way from Margam Country Park to Rhigos Mountain, the Ffordd y Bryniau (Taff Ely Ridgeway) Path between Mynydd-y-Gear and Caerphilly Common, the Ogwr Ridgeway Path and the Rhymney Valley Ridgeway.

In the eastern Valleys several local walks on high ground have been marked, such as at Cwm Celyn near Blaina (National Welsh X15, 16), Cwmtillery Lakes (National Welsh 91) and Pen-y-Fan Pond north of Crumlin (National Welsh A1, 2 plus short walk), as well as a series of village-based self-guided heritage walks such as at Nantyglo (National Welsh).

Ebbw Vale is the site of the 1992 Garden Festival which aims to bring the beauty of gardens and the countryside into town.

There is a local walk between Trefil and Rassau (National Welsh C8, 9) along a disued railway in the moorland.

Near Tredegar is Bryn Bach Park, near to the Heads of the Valleys road, an example of how a ravaged mining area can be coaxed back to parkland. Following the Sirhowy south towards Newport, you will find one of the best country parks in the Valleys, Sirhowy Valley Country Park (0495) 270991 stretching some four miles between Blackwood and Risca (National Welsh 56) with the Sirhowy Valley Walk, the Trim Trail and permanent orienteering routes in the thousand acres or so of territory. There is a programme of events and guided walks as well as Land Rover Safaris. The Ynys Hywel Countryside Centre based at the park runs environmental courses on wildlife habitat, organic gardening etc. and serves wholesome food into the bargain.

Further down the valley, near Cwmbran, are several local walks (self-guided leaflet available) around the forests of Cwmcarn (National Welsh X15, 16, 51, 53, 555 to the village), a coniferous mass broken up by fast-running streams. More interesting are the Upper Cwmbran Heritage Walks around Blaen Bran reservoir.

In and around the Rhymney Valley are dozens of good walks, particularly on the Rhymney Valley Ridgeway or to Parc Cwm Darran (C10). In the south near Caerfilli are local walks with accompanying leaflets leading up the ridges above Bedwas, Machen and Rudry. Above Caerfilli is the Ffordd-y-Bryniau or Ridgeway Walk from Hoel-y-Cwm to the Caerfilli Mountain Countryside Centre at Caerfilli Common. Guided walks are provided throughout the area by Countryside Service based at the centre.

One of the most interesting trails in the area is the Taff Valley Trail between Quakers Yard (train) and Merthyr along many stretches of Richard Trevethick's early tramroad and the Glamorganshire Canal as well as alongside the Taff. The path is broken into two sections on the eight mile route. Another interesting local project is the Morlais Heritage Self-Guided Trail which has been spearheaded by Pen-y-Dre High School and Merthyr Tydfil Groundwork Trust.

The Dare Valley, with its magnificently-restored country park near Aberdare (train), contains many marked routes and walks can be made between railway stations along the valley.

The Rhondda Valley provides good local walks particularly at Blaenrhondda (National Welsh T4) where there is a series of small waterfalls, but also into the glorious hills above traversed by the Coed Morgannwg Way.

Off the Heads of the Valley route and in the Neath Valley is a variety of beautiful countryside walks. For waterfalls and caves, Ystradfellte is a good detour (National Welsh 188), not many miles from Pontheddfechan Tourist Information Centre. Another detour to Coelbren (South Wales Transport) will bring you to the Henrhyd Falls, a spectacular drop of 90 feet. There are dozens of other local walks in the area, to Melin Cwrt waterfall, the old gunpowder factory walk, or the Dinas silica mines trail.

Approaching Neath, there are walks along the Neath Canal from Aberdulais Basin and at Aberdulais Falls.

Further south, Afan Argoed Country Park (South Wales Transport X1, 2, 36) in the Afan Valley offers miles of local walks in and out of the valley which was once home to the actor Richard Burton.

**Museums:** The Valleys, as one would expect, are rich in industrial heritage. At Pontypool, Junction Cottage (0495) 752036 is an old tollkeeper's cottage near Pontypool railway station that houses an exhibition about local waterways. Not far away is the Valley Inheritance telling the tale of Torfaen Valley; it is near Pontypool bus station. The Blaenafon Ironworks is the best example of a late eighteenth-century ironworks in Western Europe and The Big Pit at Blaenafon is a very authentic underground working (0495) 790311.

In the Merthyr area, the Ynysfach Engine House (0685) 83704 explains the growth of the area as a world leader in the production of iron. Also in the town is the birthplace of the musician and composer, Joseph Parry. A short bus ride (National Welsh) out of Merthyr is the Cyfartha Castle Museum, an ironmaster's house now illustrating life in the time of early industrialisation.

In the Rhondda valley, the Rhondda Heritage Park reconstructs life as it was in the valley when coal production dominated all else. To the south is the only major castle site in the Valleys, Caerphilly Castle. Nearby in the Rhymney Valley is Llancaiach Fawr, a sixteenth-century manor house reflecting local history during the period of the English Civil War.

In the valley of the Dulais, a tributary of the Neath, is the Cefn Colliery Museum, a pit museum housed in the original buildings.

**Bookshops:** Natural Selection in Glebelands Street, Merthyr has a small Green book section, as does Morgan Jones, Cardiff Road,

Caerphilly. The Blaenafon Bookshop, Broad Street, Blaenafon; Rowlands in Blackwood; Bookends in Pontypool; the Strand Bookshop and Beacon Books in Cwmbran, all have local books.

**Craft workshops:** A number of craftspeople work in the Valleys, many on new industrial estates. They include Kingmaker Coal Sculpting at the Rhondda Craft Centre, Trehafod, and people making traditional miners' safety lamps at Aberdare. Mid Glamorgan County Council produces a leaflet indicating places of work open to the public.

**Wholefood:** Natural Selection, Glebelands Street, Merthyr Tydfil offers a selection of healthy foods. Johnsons Delicatessen in the High Street also sells good food. Beanfreaks, Caradoc Road, Cwmbran sells a wide range of wholefood. The Health Food Shop at Risca sells a range of food, as does the Wholefood and Health Shop, Cardiff Road, Caerphilli. The Courthouse Restaurant in Caerphilli sells good food including Caerphilli cheese made on the premises.

Neath Health Stall, Market Hall, Neath sells wholefoods.

**Co-operatives:** The Red Flannel Theatre Group (0443) 480564 is based at Pontypridd. If you require a taxi, Independent Taxi Service (Pencoed) Ltd. (0656) 864220 are available.

**Community initiatives:** Groundwork Trust (0685) 73700 in Glebelands Street, Merthyr Tydfil, is working with the community and local businesses on environmental improvement schemes.

Merthyr Heritage Trust, Ynysfach Engine House, Merthyr (0685) 83704 is a registered charity working to secure the preservation and restoration of historical sites in the area.

The Merthyr Tydfil and Cynon Valley Ramblers Association programme is usually available at local libraries.

There is a Vegan Community Project based in the Valleys. Contact Mr. B. Howes, Caerau, Maesteg, Bridgend.

South East Wales Arts Association, Victoria Street, Cwmbran encourages community involvement in the arts.

Cynon's Best Community Arts, Abernant-y-Groes House, Bridge Road, Cwmbach, Aberdare is committed to focusing on and developing the very best of the Cynon Valley's cultural traditions and making them available to everyone.

## Suggestions for future editions of this Guide.

Please use this page, or a separate letter, to make suggestions for inclusions in, or deletions from, the next edition of the *Green Guide to Wales*.

I recommend the inclusion of:

I recommend the deletion of:

(Please give full names and addresses, and state the reasons for your recommendation.)

Name: . . . . . . . . . . . . . . . . . . . . . . . . . . . . . . . . . . . . . . . . . . . . . . . . . . . . . . . . . . .
Address: . . . . . . . . . . . . . . . . . . . . . . . . . . . . . . . . . . . . . . . . . . . . . . . . . . . . . . . . .
. . . . . . . . . . . . . . . . . . . . . . . . . . . . . . . . . . . . . . . . . . . . . . . . . . . . . . . . . . . . . . . .
Phone: . . . . . . . . . . . . . . . . . . . . . . . . . . . . . . . . . . . . . . . . . . . . . . . . . . . . . . . . . . .

Return this form to GG Wales, c/o Green Print, 10 Malden Road, London NW5 3HR.